## THE ATLANTIC STANDUP PADDLE CROSSING – 93 DAYS ALONE AT SEA

# CHRIS BERTISH

'To cross an ocean alone requires real courage. Getting to the other side takes huge resilience. To conceive of such a journey in the first place, you need incredible self-belief. Chris Bertish has them all.'
- Lewis Pugh - Endurance swimmer and UN Patron of the Oceans

'Chris Bertish is always totally committed to the various extreme challenges he assigns himself, and does them in full support of other people's needs. I've watched in awe for a number of years as Chris selflessly uses his time and skills to bring awareness to various causes dear to him and many others.'
- Kelly Slater - Eleven times Surfing World Champion

'There is a fine line between remarkable and crazy. Read this book to find out which side of the line Chris is on and how you can be on that side too.'
- Guy Kawasaki - Author, host of the *Remarkable People* podcast, past Chief Evangelist at Apple & now of Canva.

'After reading this account, I conclude that Chris's Atlantic crossing ranks as one of the great expeditions and achievements in the history of exploration!'
- Professor Timothy Noakes - Sports Scientist, Nutrition guru: Sports Scientist- (MBChB) MD + DSC (Med)

'Chris is the truest definition of what is possible when we believe in ourselves. From winning at one of the fiercest big waves on the planet, Mavericks, to his solo adventures across the world's largest oceans. Thank you Chris for showing us that we all can live our own Heroes Journey.'
- Kai Lenny - Professional Big Wave Surfer, SUP Champion & Waterman

'Nothing comes close to what Chris Bertish accomplished in his transatlantic SUP crossing. This 93-day solo expedition is the single most impactful and inspirational journey to ever occur in the history of stand up paddling. Period.'
- Evelyn O'Doherty - Chief Editor - *StandUp Journal / Session*

*It matters not how strait the gate,*
  *How charged with punishments the scroll,*
*I am the master of my fate:*
  *I am the captain of my soul.*
– William Ernest Henley, 'Invictus'


*And once the storm is over, you won't remember how you made it through, how you managed to survive. You won't even be sure, whether the storm is really over. But one thing is certain. When you come out of the storm, you won't be the same person who walked in. That's what this storm's all about.*
– Haruki Murakami, *Kafka on the Shore*


*Only those who will risk going too far, can possibly find out how far one can go!*
– T. S. Eliot

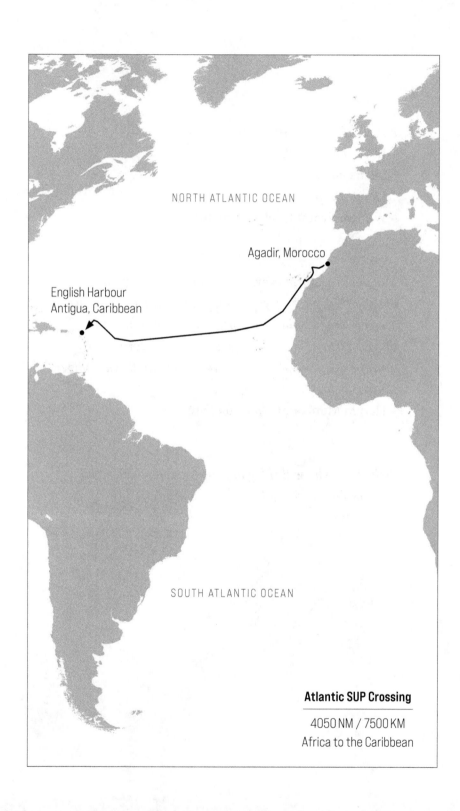

NORTH ATLANTIC OCEAN

Agadir, Morocco

English Harbour
Antigua, Caribbean

SOUTH ATLANTIC OCEAN

**Atlantic SUP Crossing**

4050 NM / 7500 KM
Africa to the Caribbean

# Distance Measurements

**NM – nautical mile** – The nautical mile is based on the Earth's latitude and longitude coordinates, with one nautical mile equaling one minute of latitude. A nautical mile is slightly longer than a mile on land, equaling 1,1508 land-measured (or statute) miles.

**sm – statute mile** – The familiar land mile is called a statute mile. It is based on paces and is 5,280 feet, or 1,609 kilometers.

**km – kilometers** – there are 1,852 meters, or 1,852 kilometers in a nautical mile. To travel around the Earth at the equator, you would have to travel 21,600 nautical miles, 24,857 miles or 40,003 kilometers.

**kn – knots** – one knot equals one NM per hour (or 1,15 statute miles per hour).

*Chris Bertish covered 4050 NM/7500 km on his solo Atlantic crossing.*

# Nautical Terms

**Bow** – The front of the craft or boat.

**Stern** – The back of the craft or boat.

**Port** – If you are looking forward to the bow of any boat/yacht, the port side would be the left hand side.

**Starboard** – If you are looking forward to the bow of any boat/yacht, the starboard side would be the right hand side.

**The deck** – The top side of the craft that I stand on and paddle from, between the stern area and the front pod (my cabin).

**Trades / trade winds** – The winds over a certain section of the Atlantic and Pacific oceans that are normally fairly consistent in strength and direction are commonly known as the trades; they blow in the same direction, every year over that area of ocean.

**Para-anchor / parachute anchor** – The sea anchor that I deploy off the side of the craft when the weather is bad, in order to get dragged slowly with the ocean conditions to slow down and stabilize the craft and drift ratio. It looks like a parachute – 6 feet wide, and attached to a line 20 meters long, which connects to the front of my craft. I retrieve it with another line called the retrieval line, which I pull it back in with, onto the side of the craft, where it is stuffed into a small bag on deck, waiting to be deployed again.

**Waypoint** – A particular position on an ocean chart indicated by a GPS point, which is given by a latitude and longitude coordinate to give the exact location. A route on the ocean is often made up of a sequence of waypoints.

**GPS** – Global Positioning System, uses a device that gives your exact position in coordinates, also using latitude and longitude, via an array of orbiting satellites.

# Contents

# Foreword

When I had completed the foreword to Chris Bertish's first book, *Stoked!*, I presumed that this would be the end. For the book described enough quests to fill a legion of lives; surely there was no need for yet more explorations.

The defining moment in Stoked! occurred during the 2010 Mavericks Big Wave Invitational surfing competition in Half Moon Bay, California. The event featured the most monstrous waves – in excess of 50 foot – in the history of competitive surfing. Given only 36 hours to travel from Cape Town to San Francisco; arriving just three hours before the competition began and with his board and wetsuit lost en route, in his first heat Chris was held down under multiple 60-foot waves, experiencing a near fatal drowning. His choice became to retire gracefully from the competition. Or to continue. He chose to continue. Later that afternoon after surfing another five monster waves in the semi-finals and finals, Chris was crowned the winner of what will forever be remembered as perhaps the most epic competition in surfing history.

Having once been scared rigid surfing a rather less gigantic six-foot wave I realized that, although we inhabit the same city, Chris and I exist in different universes.

When Chris informed me that he was planning to cross the Atlantic alone on a tiny stand-up paddleboard, I was quite certain that there would be no sequel to *Stoked!*. For in my more limited universe the probability that Chris could survive a paddle of 7500 kilometers across the Atlantic Ocean on his own, was infinitesimally small. The certainty of a fatal outcome was simply overwhelming: illness; injury; being run over by an ocean liner in the middle of the night; equipment failure; starvation from running out of food, etc. In my universe the list of dangers was simply overwhelming.

Of course in Chris's universe, the list was very much longer and, for us but not for him, even more frightening. And that is exactly why he would dare to challenge the impossible. He did not choose to cross the Atlantic because it is easy. Rather, in the words of a former US president, 'because it was hard'. Very hard. Almost, but not quite, too hard. Having now read this complete record, I conclude that his ocean crossing ranks as one of the great achievements in the history of exploration.

So how do I justify that opinion?

Some years ago I wondered what the greatest human endurance performance of all time was. This took me to the iconic Polar explorers from the beginning of the 20th Century including Nansen, Shackleton, Scott, Amundsen and, more recently, Sir Ranulph Fiennes and Dr Michael Stroud. I graded the difficulty of their performances according to the total energy they had to expend in their quests compared to modern athletes like cyclists in the 21-day Tour de France, a particularly demanding event.

The clear winner was Captain Robert Scott's team that expended more than 1 million kilocalories (kcal) in their ultimately fatal 159-day trek to and from the South Pole in the Antarctic summer of 1911/12. This compares to about 170,000 kcal expended by Tour de France cyclists, which is about half the energy cost of running across the continental United States. Of the modern Polar explorers, Fiennes and Stroud expended an estimated 570,000 kcal in their 95-day 2300 km trek across Antarctica. By the end both had lost 20 kg, had exceeded their physical limits and were close to death.

In his 93-day Atlantic crossing, Chris Bertish paddled an average of 10 hours a day, averaging 36 strokes/min for a total of 930 hours of paddling involving more than 2 million paddle strokes. The energy cost of stand-up paddling varies between 500 (light paddling) and 900 (competitive paddling) kcal/hr. A conservative measure would be that Chris expended at least 550,000 kcal in paddling across the Atlantic. Which places his performance in the same league as that of Fiennes and Stroud in their near fatal Antarctic crossing.

But as you read this epic account you will realize that by comparison the Polar explorers had it rather easier. They were walking and sleeping on a stable surface; their navigation was less complex; they were not at risk of getting irretrievably lost in an enormous ocean; they had no scarcity of water; they did not go backwards if they stopped moving forwards; they were doing what others had already done; and they had others with whom to share their mental burden. Nor was there the constant danger of falling overboard and drowning.

Sir Raymond Priestley who accompanied first Shackleton in 1909 and then Scott in 1911 to Antarctica, wrote: 'For scientific discovery give me Scott; for speed and efficiency of travel give me Amundsen; but when disaster strikes and all hope is gone, get down on your knees and pray for Shackleton.'

Perhaps if he was now alive to read this book, Priestley might revise his opinion.

Perhaps like me he would conclude: To cope effectively with all eventualities, always give me Chris Bertish.

My friend, my hero and my inspiration.

*Professor Timothy Noakes*

# PROLOGUE
# Just Add Water

Mavericks, CA | 37°29'32.97"N 122°30'8.75"W

Just add water, and everything is okay...

Everything I do has always involved water and the ocean. After winning the Mavericks Big Wave Invitational in 2010, in the biggest waves ever paddled into at the time, I needed a new challenge, a new ocean sport to push my limits. I found it in stand-up paddleboarding.

Stand-up paddleboarding combines all my water sports experience – windsurfing, surfing, and sailing – with a greater understanding of the ocean and the elements. It's the most versatile sport I know. I love the fact that I can still ride big waves on my stand-up paddleboard (SUP), but at the same time, use it to explore coastlines, rivers, waterfalls – and create my own adventures.

Naturally, I always wanted to push it further.

One day I was chatting with some friends around a fire.

'What if I could use only the strength in my arms and the skills I've learned across all the sports, over all my years as a waterman and use all of this knowledge and experience to paddle solo, completely unsupported, all the way across the Atlantic Ocean, from one continent to another?' I asked.

'That's impossible,' they said.

'Is it?' I smiled.

# 'All In'

What would you put on the line, give up or sacrifice for what you believe in?

People talk about being 'All In', but often it's just a loose expression implying that they are committed to something, but they're not actually prepared to put much on the line.

For me, the definition of 'All In' is being totally committed. It's being prepared to put everything in your life on the line for what you believe in – no matter what! It's about letting go, shedding your skin, freeing yourself from material things and everything you have accumulated in order to follow your passions, because you believe in it with every fiber in your being and are prepared to do whatever it takes to achieve something greater than yourself.

'All In', in its purest sense, is a state that I have lived all my life. It's the reason for every success in everything I have done.

Another is something I call 'Visual Blueprinting'. If you've read my previous book *Stoked!* you'll know my mantra *See it, Dream it, Believe it, Achieve it.*

Visualization is the key that unlocks this process. I've used visualization, manifestation and visual imaging in all my biggest projects and to achieve my greatest goals – not just in sport, but in all areas of my life.

The way it works is this: I imagine every detail of the thing I am striving for, until I can see it so clearly it's like being able to watch the movie in my head over and over, in full HD.

I imagine it so completely that I can see the colors: vivid, raw and rich. I hear the sounds, smell the scents in the sea air, see the water in perfect motion... Once I can play it in moving color with sight and sound, I start adding the emotion, which is the purpose, my 'why'.

Those feelings are like rocket fuel – pure power. When it gets really tough out there, you need this fuel to keep you going, it becomes your superpower.

Some things are so epic you can't even imagine them. I never imagined that I would get towed towards the cliffs of the Canary Islands by a giant sea squid; or surf down 10-meter waves in the middle of the Atlantic, hanging on the edge of my modified SUP for dear life; or get breached on and circled by a giant Great White shark thousands of miles away from any help. At that point, I was actually closer to the International Space Station than to any other human!

These are the things I didn't visualize, but which all happened to me during my 7500 km transatlantic solo SUP crossing. In the pages that follow, I'll tell you all about them, how I survived them and overcame the odds to succeed in something everyone thought was simply impossible – if not totally bonkers!

I hope you enjoy the story, I hope it positively impacts on your life, like it has mine, that you will be inspired and possibly have your horizons widened and your perceptions of what is possible in your own life altered forever.

Remember, the only way forward is *All In*!

# Just Start!

The Molokai is a 31-mile (51-km) race from Molokai to Oahu, Hawaii, against the world's best stand-up paddlers. It's known to be the most grueling, most difficult, and longest stand-up paddleboard race in the world. Entries are strictly limited to 80 participants. In 2015, because I held the 12-hour SUP World Record, I was invited to be one of them.

It was something I'd wanted to do ever since I first heard about it. The timing wasn't ideal, just two weeks after my 24-hour Open Ocean Record, but I felt privileged to be part of it and was keen to see where I stood in relation to the world's top SUP paddlers.

We were going to be showing *Ocean Driven*, my film about my 2010 Mavericks win, at one of the main cinemas on Oahu. So a couple days before registration for Molokai, my wife Clellind and I flew out, attended the screening, and then flew over to Maui the following day.

I wasn't able to bring my own ocean race board because of its length. The board I had done all my records on was a 17-foot 'bullet', a pretty standard size for this kind of race, but not one that airlines will accommodate.

One of my sponsors, SIC, was based in Maui and said they would provide me with a board for the race. Sadly, when I arrived there it turned out they didn't have a 17-foot board, only a 14-foot – not what I was used to, but since I was technically on honeymoon, I just accepted it, I was happy to compete and see how I would do.

It turned out that ferries don't accept ocean race boards easily either. Special transport boats had been arranged to take all the race participants' boards from Maui to the start point of the race at Molokai, but by the time I got there with my borrowed board, they had all left for the island. The last ferry was for passengers only; boards were definitely not allowed – the ferry driver made it clear he would get fired if he made an exception.

There was really only one option for me: put my wife on the last ferry and paddle myself over to Molokai, or miss the race.

The race from Molokai to Oahu runs across the 'Channel of Bones' – renowned for big seas, strong winds and currents. On the other side is Maui with a 29-mile wide channel – but there is more wind on that side, so most people don't do that crossing. This is the one I was about to do.

There are thousands of miles between these islands and the next one, which is Fiji, so if you don't have a support boat and you go missing, you are gone. But there was simply no other way I was going to be able to get myself and my board over there.

Most other people probably wouldn't dream of doing that channel crossing solo or alone. But for me it was a really simple solution and the only option available with a guaranteed outcome. This is what I had been training for the last couple of years – all the solo journeys I had done, in way more treacherous waters… *So just paddle it! It's that simple.*

So I just paddled the Maui-to-Molokai channel, alone and unsupported, almost the exact same distance as the actual race from Molokai to Oahu, only the afternoon before.

I did the 46-kilometer paddle in just under six hours, with all my gear and no one else around. And man, it was the most incredible crossing! It's probably still to this day the best downwind crossing I've ever done on a stand-up paddleboard anywhere on the planet. Beautiful warm, blue water, a couple of reef sharks and turtles and flying fish, and some of the most amazing runs I've ever experienced.

I got to the pier at Molokai at six o'clock that evening. I met my wife and checked into the hotel room just before the welcome function. No one else in the race knew that I'd just done one of the longest, heaviest channels in the world, completely unsupported, just to get to the race!

But if I thought the race itself was going to be easy by comparison, I was mistaken.

I managed to get a decent night's sleep and was up early in the morning for the opening ceremony and special blessing led by Clark Abbey.

Then I met up with my support boat crew. Every racer has to have his or her own support boat. We'd been through everything before so we had everything prepped. It looked like the wind would be very light across the journey, so a lot of people were worried it was going to be very hot, which could result in heat exhaustion. But since I'd done my own private Molokai the day before, I was ready to rock and roll!

I was waiting on the start line, happy to be there and just be a part of it; a dream come true. The horn went for the beginning of the race, I took three strokes… and on my third stroke, my paddle shaft snapped in my hand and came apart completely in two pieces.

This was my favorite race paddle that I'd been using for the last two and a half years through all my different journeys. Now I was standing at the start line, watching everyone else disappear off into the distance, with two pieces of paddle in my hand.

I've never, ever had a paddle snap on me before. The only other paddle I had brought with me was my wave paddle, which is completely different – it has a different blade, different strength, different flex pattern and, most importantly, it's almost two feet shorter than a proper downwind race paddle.

The race rules stipulated that if there was any problem on the start line, no one could call in backup until everyone had cleared at least 200 m from the start. So I had to sit there waiting, literally watching everyone disappear off into the distance before I could even try and find my team amongst the hundred-odd support boats that were there. It probably took me 10 minutes before I located them and got the other paddle sorted.

At that point, I could have dropped out – just thrown in the paddle, literally. No one had ever done a Molokai with a wave paddle – never mind starting 15 minutes behind everyone else. Anybody that's paddled a SUP knows how completely different a race paddle and a wave paddle are, and what the difference of almost two feet in shaft length makes to your stroke. I just thought to myself, *Well, I'm just going to have to learn a different kind of stroke and different way of paddling on this crossing.*

Then I looked out into the distance. I was so far behind that the entire fleet had already gone around the corner. I couldn't even see them. I could literally only just make out the last competitor, one yellow jersey ahead of me.

I said to myself, *Well it's really simple. Think of that person as your 'Golden Monkey'. He's your target, and you are just going to do your damnedest to try and catch him up.*

That was my only goal: just to catch that one last person I could see with the bright golden vest on. So for the next hour, that's all I did; I just focused on trying to catch that one 'monkey'.

Amazingly, within about 45 minutes I'd caught up with him and then reset my target to the next monkey. And when I got to that monkey, I was like, *Well, now I can see lots more monkeys in the distance.* So I set my sights on the next monkey that I could find. And I caught that one. And then I caught another. And then another, and another, until I realized that I wasn't actually doing too badly, I was catching a lot of monkeys! Now my goal was to catch as many monkeys as possible.

It turned out to be one of the toughest Molokai races in the history of the race. More than 30% of the fleet pulled out because of heat exhaustion. There wasn't a lot of wind, which made it absolutely brutal. By the time I got to the iconic China Walls, the rock point just before the beach where the race finished, I had caught over 63 monkeys. And because I'd mapped out that location and knew it pretty well, and because by random chance there was a big south swell that day (super rare that time of the year) I ended up catching a wave all the way from the outside right through till just before the finish, overtaking another five monkeys on the way in.

Even though I started a couple miles behind everyone else, and paddled with a wave paddle and a stock standard 14-foot board, I still ended up making the top five in my division.

It just goes to show that if you put your head down, focus on what's in front of you, break it down and just pick off one monkey at a time, you can achieve anything. That's my Law of the Golden Monkeys.

I believe that everyone needs their own monkeys to keep them going; goals on their journey and a golden monkey they may never catch, but which keeps them going even when the going gets tough. *Especially* when the going gets tough. It's called being driven by passion and powered by purpose.

It's what helped get me across the Atlantic Ocean just over a year later.

# Back to the Beginning

I like to keep learning and growing and trying new things. Stand-up paddleboarding was no exception – but it made me realize I'm a lot more competitive than I thought.

Whenever I get into a new sport I become super passionate about it – obsessively focused, some would say, until I've got it down to a point that I feel I'm well skilled at it.

In 2012, I started to get obsessive about stand-up paddleboarding. I was in Cape Town, and I started riding big waves at my local breaks – Sunset and Crayfish Factory. Even taking supping to another level by getting barreled at Dungeons, our local, very scary big wave.

I finally got a big wave SUP made by my great friend and legend, Jeff Clark, and started riding locations all over the world, including Mavericks. I became the first person to stand-up paddle into Nelscott Reef in Oregon and got caught inside by some really big waves.

While all that was happening, I was also starting to get into open-ocean downwind stand-up paddleboarding. It was sort of like all the water sports I'd ever done combined; it connected the dots between sailing, surfing and stand-up paddleboarding. The way it utilized the weather, the wind, riding the bumps and the energy of the ocean really fascinated me.

Basically, because you are standing up, your body acts as a sail, which means downwind is a lot easier than going into the wind. So I started to do all the downwind runs in South Africa around Cape Town, distances of between 10 and 20km. At the same time I was also doing SUP wave riding, trying to juggle surfing on the Big Wave World Tour, while running a business full time, to pay the bills.

In order to be successful at anything, you have to challenge your-self constantly and tackle things head on. So even though I was very accomplished in big wave surfing, I wanted to lean into a new sport. I wanted to challenge myself, evolve and grow through to something else. And I think you can use that principle on anything, not just sport, if you go 'All In'.

Following your heart, creating a burning desire, gives you the passion to keep going and keep pushing through the tough times. Fear can be a positive thing too. When you move through your fears and tackle them head on... that's where the magic happens, and where your greatest potential lies. That's when we are forced to lift our game and become the best versions of ourselves. That's when we shine and live our greatest life.

So, I started really getting into downwind stand-up paddleboard, doing downwind runs with 30 to 40 knots of wind across an 8-mile (12-km) distance downwind. I became the first SUP to join the local surfski race every Wednesday night; within a year I was beating the back third of the surfski fleet.

I held the record as South Africa's top downwind stand-up paddle-boarder or three or four years and was part of the team that repre-sented SA in the ISA SUP World Championships in 2012 and 2013. I started comparing my times with the guys overseas and found that I had some of the fastest times in the world over the long distances. That got me thinking about the 12-hour record, which was just over 60 miles (96 km). So I started looking for a section of coastline where I could do 100 or 110 km over two days.

This was a long time before I had the idea to stand-up paddle solo across the Atlantic Ocean. But the germ of the idea was there, in those hours of being alone at sea, just me and my board.

Before I could even come up with the pitch, I had to prove it could be done.

That started the idea for the expedition I called the 'Proof of Concept'.

# Proof-of-Concept Paddle

Cape Point, RSA | 34°21'16.47"S 18°28'13.80"E

For most of 2012, I was thinking of how to cross the Atlantic on a SUP. I figured out the way to do it was to go from Senegal to Brazil, which is probably the shortest route, and planned on using a support boat. I even launched the idea that October, at The Toad – my good friend Dougie Boyes's restaurant. I told everybody my plan, but I didn't really get any buy in or positive feedback. Pretty much everyone thought it was impossible. And if you know anything about me, you'll know that word doesn't ever sit well with me. It's like a red rag to a bull.

The more I researched the idea, the more I realized that the greatest challenge and expense would actually be for a support boat. You need a boat that is nimble enough to come alongside you in unpredictable seas, but big enough to handle the distance. It needs to be able to stop, start, and return to a specific GPS position after each shift, daily and through the night, through all conditions, rain, shine or storm, for more than three months. That suddenly became a totally different logistical challenge, because the type of vessel you needed to do all that, was a very big, 65 ft-plus, expensive yacht or research vessel, built to withstand long durations at sea. That narrows things down to a very unique vessel, that costs an untenable amount of money. You are also 100% reliant on them; if anything goes wrong with that vessel or crew and they need to return to land for whatever reason, your expedition is over!

So then I thought, *What if I could do it without a support boat?* What if I could build the right little craft so I could carry everything I needed – dehydrated food, watermaker, navigational and comms equipment – and be completely self sufficient?

I needed to do a proof-of-concept paddle, which would be to paddle, unsupported, over 350 km (220 miles) – about a tenth of the shortest distance across the Atlantic, from Senegal to Brazil. If I could do that, and possibly do a 12-hour open-ocean record to show that I could handle the relentlessness of the task, then I could prove that it was possible and I'd be able to give it a crack. So that's pretty much what I set out to do for the next year.

■ ■ ■

The West Coast of South Africa is known as one of the gnarliest coastlines in the world. The water rarely gets above 14°C (57°F), the winds are notoriously ferocious, consistently blowing over 40 kn, through the summer, with seas that are big and wild and there are plenty of sharks. The infamous Cape of Storms, which is a graveyard of shipwrecks, is known globally as one of the world's most treacherous coastlines, and if you can learn to survive in these conditions, you can survive pretty much anywhere and any ocean conditions on the planet.

So I mapped out a 350 km stretch from Cape Point in the south (the second most southern point of Africa) to Lamberts Bay in the north, up the Atlantic West Coast.

This was to be a solo mission, which meant carrying everything I needed on the board: tent, sleeping bag, cooking gear, food, hydration, communication equipment, emergency, first aid and safety gear. Everything had to be watertight and strapped down to my SUP, meticulously, with backups of most of the main critical safety devices. It all added up to over 40 kg, strapped down onto my 17 ft Naish Javelin.

Finally the day came and I was ready. The forecast looked promising with steady southeast trades predicted, which should have given me epic downwind conditions for most of the way. Should have is the key phrase there… because they didn't.

Leaving from Cape Point was the first challenge. The heaving five-meter surf that week was causing havoc along the entire coastline. It made it almost impossible to get out through the surf and across the outer reefs. It was ridiculous to try and get through those conditions, even with nothing on your board, but with all my gear strapped down there was just no way I could do it safely and survive. After three or four attempts I moved about two kilometers north, to Olifantsbos. I knew the channels from surfing here and managed to sneak out, watched by ostriches on the beach, some gemsbok and a few baboons.

Paddling just under 40 km that day I went past Scarborough, Kommetjie, Hout Bay, and Dungeons – one of Cape Town's premier big wave spots and I was very mindful of those big four- to five-meter waves and gave it a wide berth. It didn't help that a giant sunfish just off Dungeons scared the living hell out of me – the fin sticking out of the water looks just like a giant Great White shark!

I spent the first night at Sandy Bay, setting my alarm for 4 am to be on the water between 5 and 6 am. On day two I woke up to a howling 35-kn offshore wind. It was not supposed to be that strong, but luckily it backed off by 8 am – I had to cover 40 km to Robben Island, where Nelson Mandela was imprisoned for so many years. You're not allowed to stay there, but I figured if I got close in the late afternoon, I could skirt the back end of the island and come in under the mask of darkness. So that's what I did. As the sun began to set I came in amongst all the kelp beds to camouflage myself, pulled all my gear up through a penguin colony and set up my camp hidden amongst the bushes, with the most amazing view of Table Mountain lit up by the city lights. It was one of the most special and unique nights under the stars in my life.

I woke up super early because I needed to be gone by first light, not to be seen by the rangers. Day three was probably my biggest paddle day: a monster 52 km to Dassen Island. That's like paddling more than a Molokai Race, open-ocean, 10–20 km offshore, but with NO support or support boat, in far more testing and severe conditions, in icy Atlantic water, with the equivalent in weight of a small human tied to the deck of your board.

The journey between Robben Island and Dassen Island had never been paddled before. I would be between eight and fifteen kilometers off the coastline, and if I got it wrong and missed the island for any reason and got blown out, the closest form of land after that point is Brazil! I wasn't quite ready to cross the Atlantic just yet, and definitely not on my normal SUP!

Unfortunately the predicted SSE wind never got out of the south-west corner, which was really bad for me, as I had to paddle the entire way, paddling only on one side, with the wind 90 degrees off my left shoulder. By the time I reached the lee of the island, over 10 hours from my 6 am start, I was completely broken, fatigued, sunstroked and beyond exhausted. But I knew if I sat down, took a break at all, I'd be pushed so far off course that I wouldn't be able to make the island, so I had to just keep on paddling on one side.

At 4:45 pm I only just got to the corner of the island as the wind picked up to over 30 kn and I grabbed the first piece of kelp that I could find, just off the outer reefs. I lay there, holding on for what seemed like hours, but was probably only 20 minutes, just trying to regain my composure and my breath. My hands were blistered across all my fingers, and I was feeling deep fatigue through my muscles and bones. By the time I found a way in it was a quarter to six. I was so exhausted I just pulled all my stuff up onto the beach, collapsed face down on the sand and passed out.

When I woke up it was pitch black. I was completely dehydrated, but found some water on the island. My eyes felt scratchy and really sensitive and I was worried about how they would be in the morning. I set up my little camp, made some food, and checked in on my sat phone tracker, to let people on the mainland know I'd made it.

When I woke up on day four I could hardly open my eyes – my corneas were badly burnt. To make matters worse, a thick fog had set in down the coast, taking visibility down to less than 50 meters. To start in that mist, with a northerly headwind that would swing to the south-west, made the 55 km to Langebaan Lagoon a nightmare; it would be pushing me onto land and the surf was forecast to be massive.

About an hour in I heard engines, getting louder and louder in the middle of the fog. A lot of these fishing boats don't have any lights or safety equipment on board, so they wouldn't even know if they ran me flat. I was looking around everywhere but by now, I couldn't see more than 20 meters in front of me. It was absolutely terrifying. Eventually the engines went away; the vessel had obviously gone past.

I started to get really disoriented, with white everywhere around me. I checked my GPS and my paper charts to make sure I was going in the right direction – the wind felt like it was on the wrong side. Then I started hearing this really weird noise. I didn't know what it was, but it started getting louder and more consistent. Just when I thought I must be hallucinating, a big humpback whale came up out of the fog right next to me!

Then another one came up and blew its spout. And then another. There was a pod of 15 or 20 whales surrounding me. I just stopped in awe of these incredible creatures. When they are swimming underneath and around you, there's an amazing connection that's hard to describe. I felt like they were guiding me.

I double-checked my GPS and charts and found I was actually going in the wrong direction. Then the fog started lifting and I realized that the whales seemed to be guiding me back towards land. I made a change in direction and the whales swam with me for another 10 minutes or so and then disappeared. It was an incredible experience.

I had a side-wind the entire way once again, with a huge 5-metre swell. The last 25 kilometers of coastline was massive rocky cliffs with zero place to go in, so I really couldn't afford to get it wrong.

The wind picked up in a southwesterly direction and started pushing me towards the coastline. With about eight kilometers still to go the cliffs were getting scarily close. I could feel these giant swells coming underneath me and see them detonating on the rocks.

The sea state was absolutely terrifying. I was quickly running out of space and I knew I didn't have time to call the NSRI (National Sea Rescue Institute) to come and get me.

It was touch and go, mentally; that last corner, which was still two or three kilometers away, felt like there should be a big ocean sign along the stretch with blinking red lights saying 'Enter only at your own peril!'

I gobbled down a bar of chocolate and just pulled as hard as I could. I literally gave it everything that I had, and finally got around the corner and came into the mouth of Langebaan Lagoon. There I got my first downwind for the entire trip, after four grueling days, for the 4 km run down into Saldanha Bay Harbour.

By the time I got my stuff out of the water, I was so fatigued I couldn't even see straight. I realized my eyes were burnt really badly and my feet were blistering. The sun was becoming a massive problem. I decided to make day five a rest day and found a doctor to give me antibiotic drops for my eyes. They would just stream with water every time I opened them, and I couldn't look into the light.

Day six resumed, early. I packed up in the dark, contemplating another 50 km paddle around Shelley Point into St Helena Bay. My brother Greg joined me to paddle the first 20 km to a place called Jacobs Bay, and I continued on to Stompneus Bay by myself. Once again, the wind didn't play along – I had a light headwind the entire way.

Day seven's objective was make a bee-line right across the bay from Stompneus Bay to Elands Bay, a place I knew well from surfing. The West Coast is known for its microclimates. As I was paddling across the bay anticipating the south wind, it swung around and became a direct onshore – the opposite of what was forecast. Are you starting to see a pattern here with forecasts? At 15–20 kn it was another side-winder from hell.

I still had 23 km to go to Elands Bay when I realized that there was no way I was going to be able to keep paddling across it; the wind got stronger and I wasn't going to be able to keep myself offshore if I left it too late. It's a super rocky coastline and very arid, with no road access and no one around for miles, so I got to the point where I had to make the call. I knew it was dangerous for me, with all my gear strapped down on my board, but I had no other choice, I was going to have to pick a spot where there was a gap in the rocks and a sandy beach section and just go in through the surf.

The swell was still four meters. To ride in on that with a 17-foot stand-up is a task in itself, let alone when you have 40 kilograms of gear. I sat down just before I got to the surf line, put on my life jacket and strapped everything else down super tight. I managed to time the sets wisely and ride halfway in on one, before I got rolled. I lost my hat, one of my water hydration packs and a couple of other valuables. When I got up onto the beach I collected what gear I could find washed up on the sand, set up camp on the beach and looked at the forecast for the next morning.

If the wind stayed at this intensity there was absolutely no way I would be able to get off the beach. I'd lost some water and food, so now I was on severe rations. I was shipwrecked, and I still had another roughly 20 km to go before I even got to Elands Bay.

That evening I had my last bit of food. I had one energy bar left and half a two-liter bladder of water. I'd lost my hat so things weren't looking good. I just prayed that when I woke up in the morning, the wind, the sea state and the waves would have dropped enough to allow me to get out through the surf. I needed to paddle out before the wind changed and pushed me in the wrong direction again.

I knew that the wind was going to blow onshore again from 10 am onwards, so I mapped out a route and put a new waypoint in my GPS. I worked out the angles on the chart so that I could paddle out and offshore, just over eight kilometers (about five miles) off the coastline, so when I got to the waypoint about 30 kilometers away from Elands Bay, when the wind picked up in the onshore direction, that I could still come in to Lamberts Bay with the wind mostly on my back.

I knew this last day, day eight, would probably be my longest day. I got up at 4:30 am, collected all my gear and strapped it onto my board. I couldn't really see the surf yet. The first time I tried to get out, I didn't make it, and the second time neither, but the third time I managed to punch through. I got two more hours of paddling in before the wind started picking up significantly, to a point that I couldn't keep my course. I started getting pushed sideways, but by this time my angles were pretty much spot on to do the last five kilometers into Lamberts Bay with the wind mostly behind me.

When I finally came in to Lamberts Bay there was no one there to meet me because no one thought I was going make it. My team – Pete Peterson and Clells – were busy going up and down the coast looking for me. I found a little restaurant in the harbor and ordered a burger and a beer, which I couldn't even sip because of the blisters on my lips. I was fatigued and sunburnt after eight days and 350 kilometers, paddling six to ten hours each day. The good news was we raised enough money for The Lunchbox Fund charity to be able to feed 300 kids.

Not only that, but this Proof-of-Concept paddle showed that, if I built a craft that could take all my gear and allow me to get out of the sun and the elements during peak times of the day, and if I managed myself, my hydration, nutrition and sun exposure correctly, I could not only do 350 kilometers, but I could possibly paddle across an ocean.

# Serious Training: Source-to-Sea and Channel

English Channel, UK | 51°7'9.91"N 1°19'1.03"E

After the Proof-of-Concept paddle I knew it was possible to cross the Atlantic solo and unsupported. But I also knew it was going to take everything to get to the starting line: the funding to build the craft and even more so, a hell of a lot of training to get me fit, fine-tune my craft, prepare myself, physically, mentally and emotionally, and learn everything I could from these micro expeditions along the way.

Little did I know at the time it would take me three more years of training and preparation. In the process I would set and break some records, and develop a new motivational strategy: Catching the Golden Monkeys. (Disclaimer: no real monkeys were involved.)

Straight after the POC paddle I was headed to the UK to meet my client Gul International (my agency was the distributor for their wet-suits and accessories in South Africa), and so I decided to use that opportunity to SUP from the source of the River Thames to the sea. It had been done before as a run, swim and cycle, but no one had done it running, stand-up paddleboarding and cycling. The distance was just under 300 km, and I wanted to see if it was possible to do it in under four-and-a-half days.

I consulted Professor Tim Noakes regarding whether I could do it non-stop without sleeping. He told me that after 20 to 30 hours, my body would start shutting down, so I'd need to take micro naps. I wanted to test that theory – and to try to fit in doing an English Channel crossing at the same time. Neither of these are small feats, and both require huge logistical preparation in advance.

I also had to contend with a flare-up of an old injury. I hadn't run any sort of distance since I'd broken my knee 12 years before; in 2000 they told me I would never be able to run again. For the Source-to-Sea I would need to do a 21-kilometer run – a half marathon.

A couple months before I left for the expedition, I went for a five-km test run. About three quarters of the way through it felt like my knee popped, and afterwards it became really sore. I went to get X-rays and was told that the titanium wires in my knee had snapped – which apparently shouldn't be possible. If I tried any more running, they said, those wires would stick into my muscle and become excruciatingly painful – unless they operate immediately. I couldn't go for surgery, as I had to leave that week – so just decided to see if I could pull it off. All I could really do was work through the pain and practice methods to distract my mental state, learn and grow from it. As soon as I got back, I promised my surgeon, I'd get all the wires removed.

And so, 10 days later, in August 2013, I found myself in the beautiful lush green Cotswolds, under an old ash tree, 20 km from Cricklade, the first downstream town on the Thames. From here I was able to launch my SUP board into the river – with barely enough water to float.

My aim was to paddle over 90 km each day, sleeping less than three hours a day, paddling night and day for 16–20 hours, and complete the challenge in 60 hours. It took a lot longer.

One thing I hadn't counted on was having to carry all my gear up and over the many locks (almost 50 of them), which weren't open during the night. Unexpected strong headwinds didn't help either.

My good English friend Ben Grenata agreed to meet me at the different checkpoints, where I was going to change disciplines. He dropped me off that first early morning, and I ran up into the Cotswolds to find this beautiful big stone declaring the official source of the River Thames (even though there is no water to be found anywhere near it). That carved rock has been there for centuries; to be part of that history and start my run from there felt incredible.

After about 10 km my knee started becoming really painful. About five kilometers away from the point where I could switch out and start to paddle I could actually see the wires poking up against the skin. I was worried they were going to break through the surface! I was so happy to meet Ben at the switch-out point, because I could barely walk, let alone run. I rested for five minutes and then got straight onto my board.

The water was only three or four inches deep and the stream was super overgrown with reeds and trees for the first couple of kilometers. There were areas where I had to walk with my SUP, or get down on my belly and pull my way under branches. It was only after about six hours of pretty crazy foliage navigation that I could actually start paddling freely.

I spent the first night at Newbridge. It was only then that I realized that the charts and the maps for the river only show the major locks, but there were many, many more – one every two to three kilometers, in fact, which meant 15 different locks that first night. Some of them 10 to 25 feet (13 meters) high – it's pretty amazing to go through and have the water drop down by 20 feet before they open up on the other side. But if they were closed, which 90% of them were, I had to climb up and pull all my gear and my board over them.

Every now and then I was fortunate to be let through by a kind lock keeper, but by the time I got to the tenth lock, it was getting dark. My body was literally shutting down, so I just stopped on the side of the river and, keeping one leg on my board to stop it floating away, slept on the ground next to it.

I slept for 45 minutes, woke up freezing cold, and carried on going. I was so tired I actually started hallucinating, but it was still amazing going through the little towns, chatting to people walking on the riverbank, or to the geese and ducks in the water.

Sometimes I'd stop to have a quick swim. On the second day, it turned out I was in an area where the water was pretty badly polluted and I ended up getting diarrhea, so not only was I paddling for 24 hours non-stop, but I was also getting dehydrated. I lost about five kilograms in four days.

I got to Putney Bridge at 8:15 pm, after paddling over 243 km and having four power naps in three days.

The Port Authority told me it was illegal to paddle from Tower Bridge because there's too much river traffic, so this was where I'd have to bring my craft out of the water and do the last 35 km by bike.

I thought that last part was going to be easy; it wasn't. Within two hours, I had two flat tires, and no second backup puncture repair kit, so I hired a Boris bike – one of those funny little ones with a basket on the front. Even so, with much of central London Thames Path closed and gated at night, I could only reach the Thames Barrier the following day.

When I finally got there it was raining. I had a chance to repair my other puncture and changed back over to my normal bike, but it had all taken a lot longer than planned. Ben, my trusty friend and support crew, had to head back to attend a wedding, so I celebrated the first ever Thames River Source-to-Sea Run/SUP/Cycle on my own. It took me 3,5 days, 321 km, and 9,5 hours sleep to complete.

It turned out I wouldn't get much rest before the next adventure either.

I popped a bottle of champagne at the Thames Barrier and had a couple of sips to celebrate the end. Then I got back on my bike and rode to Putney, where my van with all my stuff was parked. It started to rain quite heavily, so I pulled into a little pub and ordered a beer. That's when I got an alert on my phone.

I'd booked three different potential days/slots with my support-boat pilot for the Channel crossing, because the weather and tides across the English Channel are so volatile; the two later windows were looking terrible and the only other slot I had booked that was still available was the next morning, at first light – in 12 hours' time!

I'd thought I would have at least 36 hours to recover after my Source-to-Sea, but it had taken 24 hours longer than I'd anticipated. It was now 5:30 pm, with less than 12 hours before I was set to start the crossing and I still needed to get to Dover! I called a taxi to come pick me up with my bike, got a lift to my rental van, and put all my gear inside. Then I walked across the road to the supermarket, got some pasta salads, energy and rehydration drinks, got back to the car, changed from my cycling gear into jeans and a t-shirt, sent a message to the pilot that I would meet them in the morning, and started the three-hour drive to Dover.

I got to Dover at 10:45 pm, just as the last little hotel was closing for the night. They let me in and I prepped my equipment, nutrition and hydration until 12:30 that night. I woke at 5:30 am, had a couple of bananas and some coffee, and drove down to meet the pilot and the boat that would support my crossing.

The weather window looked really good for the day; light and variable with not too strong a current. I knew I would probably never get this opportunity again. Sometimes, whether the timing isn't right and regardless of how you feel, you just have to grab an opportunity and give it your best shot. Whatever is meant to be is meant to be.

We can always find excuses for why we can't, but you just need to focus on one reason why you can and make it happen. If you can deal with it, you can learn from it. It may not work out the way you want it to, but you never know unless you try. So less than 12 hours from finishing my Source-to-Sea journey, I started the Channel crossing from Dover.

The goal was to try and do it in five hours and 10 minutes. The world record was five hours and 38 minutes. I couldn't get out in France, so I had to turn around in the middle of the Channel and come back. Despite having to stop and wait for three different ships to pass, and doing an extra mile just to make sure we were well over the halfway mark before turning around, I ended up making it back to Dover in five hours 26 minutes, which was 12 minutes off the old world record. So I set a new record, clocking an average speed of 7,1 km/hr. Fortune favors the brave and those who have the courage to just start and try, no matter what!

# Make and Break Some Records

Langebaan, RSA | 33°4'18.44"S 17°54'20.02"E

The next big preparation paddle for my Atlantic crossing came just two months later, in October 2013. I wanted to see if I could pull the 69 km distance from Cape Town's V&A Waterfront to Ysterfontein, up the West Coast, in one day.

On my chosen day the conditions looked good, but the sea was going to be wild and I was going to be doing it solo with no support boat. There were never any takers to join me on these missions back in 2013.

I'd prepped all my gear and equipment the day and night before, in between appointments with clients: safety gear, hydration, nutrition, backup water hydration packs, GPS, backup GPS, VHF radio and backup VHF radio, backup tracking device and phone, all in a water-tight bag. I sent the NSRI notification of my route, what time I was leaving, and when I anticipated getting to the end location.

I was probably about five to eight kilometers out to sea, somewhere between the harbor and Robben Island, when the NSRI came out to check on me. They had got a call from someone off the waterfront area, who had seen a stand-up paddleboarder getting blown out to sea. The wind was already pumping at 25 kn, and was forecast to pick up to 35 kn over the next four hours, with a three or four meter sea state.

They asked me if I was okay, so I said yes, I was good, no stress, then they asked where I was going and I said 'Ysterfontein'. And they said, 'We're not asking where you are from, we want to know where you are going?' Again, I said, 'Ysterfontein.' There was this really long silence. Everyone on that boat knew the distance was 70 km, and that no one had ever done that journey on a SUP in those – or any other – conditions. They insisted that I get into their boat.

I refused. I told them I actually had more safety gear than most small ocean vessels with me, and that the head of the NSRI knew my route. I had personally given him a call yesterday and would confirm with him when I arrived. Eventually they left me to carry on my journey, but it was a really interesting start!

Over the next six hours, the seas got even wilder as some big open-ocean swells started merging with really strong SE summer trades. I felt pretty good after a couple of hydration stops. There was no one else anywhere to be seen and I was probably 10 km (six miles) off land. I had my knife, extra wetsuit, heavy weather jacket and some extra thermo gear to ward off hypothermia. I was testing some really good products for hydration, nutrition and sun exposure, which all helped manage my physical and mental state.

I finally got in at Ysterfontein at about 2:30 pm, pretty much spot on the ETA I had anticipated. It had taken just under seven hours and I'd covered 69,5 km – a blistering pace of just over 10 km/h with the sea at three to five meters plus and a 35 to 40 knt wind behind me. It doesn't get a lot more intense than that. It was pretty wild, keeping my balance and staying upright for seven hours straight, but good to realize how far I could travel over that period.

Langebaan in Saldanha Bay was another roughly 30 kilometers further, another third of the distance I'd just travelled. It got me thinking that with the correct planning and preparation, I could achieve that over a longer period of time, say 12 hours, or even a little bit further for a 24-hour record. So I started researching those options and putting it together.

In December 2013, I started out to set the 12-hour Guinness World Record, starting out from Kommetjie's Slangkop Lighthouse to Saldanha Bay Harbour. We started under a full moon at 7 am, escorted by multiple humpback whales, dolphins and seals.

Any world record attempt has to be meticulously logged and recorded on video and stills, so my support crew – my buddy Darren Robertson and Maleen Hoekstra, the photographers – were on a giant eight-meter rib, skippered by Franco Veeyoti, which stayed close to me for the whole journey.

I was learning what my body could endure over the long haul journeys. We'd mapped out a meticulous nutrition and hydration plan, which now included a high energy, slow-release endurance mix by Enduren, which doesn't allow you to spike your sugar levels. My hydration packs got swapped out every two hours for the first six hours, and then every hour for the last six hours, so I was carrying less weight. I also had pit stops of 10 to 15 minute intervals for the first half of the journey, every 2–4 hours, stretching to 15 to 20 minute intervals for the last six hours, as I got more fatigued.

The wind was a little lighter than I expected, on starting, but it was a beautiful morning. I set off at a blistering pace with a light 10-kn breeze behind. In the first hour we had a whole lot of humpback whales come up around us. Three or four hours in, I realized my pace was too fast, I was pushing it too hard and had to slow myself down. That's what I learned along this journey: everything that I've done in my life in the past has always been full tilt and full on, but with these longer paddle expeditions, I had to learn to throttle back; it wasn't a sprint but more like a marathon. Six to 12 hours counts as a full-on endurance event, and one thing I had to learn was to be more like the tortoise than the hare; the hare will burn itself out, but over distance, the tortoise with the philosophy 'slowly-slowly' wins the race.

Around the halfway mark the wind picked up and started to get pretty intense. At about the 75-kilometer mark I started getting cold from fatigue. When you're on a SUP, the first thing that goes when you get cold or fatigued is your balance, so I put on an extra wetsuit layer above my waist to warm me up a little bit. At the 100-kilometer mark I realized I could definitely break the record – I just had to stay upright for the last three to four hours, to get to the north entrance of Saldanha Harbour.

As we neared the harbor a massive tanker came in in front of us and we had to wait for it to pass, but we crossed the 12-hour mark and clocked in at 130,1 kilometers, a new World Record, with a 30-knot breeze, 12-foot seas, fatigue, sunstroke, hyperthermia, sheer bliss, joy, and stoke.

We also celebrated a new Guinness World Record for the longest distance open-ocean SUP with a whole lot of beers at the nearby Langebaan Yacht Club. Langebaan is my childhood home, and the place I learned everything about the ocean, so it was a fitting place to finish and celebrate another key milestone and stepping stone to the bigger expedition to come.

# 24-hours Non-Stop

Vilanculos, Mozambique | 21°59'32.12"S 35°19'57.05"E

I live by the mantra that if you believe in anything strongly enough, and believe you can do it, no matter what people say, with the right planning, preparation, perseverance and resilience, anything is possible!

I wanted to prove it was possible to paddle for 24 hours straight. We'd had almost perfect conditions for the 12-hour record, but that wasn't the case for this next paddle.

We waited months for the right 24-hour weather window: almost no wind through the night, then building slowly through the day but not very strong in the afternoon, when I'd be the most fatigued.

It was a lot more difficult to call the weather and sort all the logistics for this journey, from Cape Point past Langebaan through the night. Before giving the green light 24 hours before the start, we had to ensure our support vessel – a 50-foot fishing boat – and crew was still available. The greatest challenge was trying to make sure that they could track me and not lose sight of me during the night, because when you're 40 km (25 miles) out to sea that can be a serious problem – even with all the safeties we had in place.

We chose Tuesday, January 6, 2015. The conditions started out intense off Cape Point, with 15 to 20 kn winds and three-and-a-half meter swells, and even though the forecast said it was going to get better it just got progressively worse. I always look at everything from a safety perspective for myself and my team, and after paddling for the most difficult six hours I can ever remember, through to two o'clock in the morning, I had to make a really tough call after a wave broke over the stern of the 50-foot support vessel and almost capsized it. I was cold and fatigued and the updated forecast showed conditions remaining the same the next day. It was just heart wrenching to call it off, but definitely the right call.

You never fight the ocean when it's in that kind of state because you will always lose; the ocean is not going to wear itself out, but you certainly will. I needed to save myself to brave another day, when things would be more manageable. I reminded myself: when you don't succeed, find the lesson and the learnings in the experience. Apply it, grow from it and move forward stronger and wiser for next time. I hoped the lessons I'd learned would ensure a more positive outcome for the next 24-hour attempt, on 16 February.

■ ■ ■

We made some key changes for round two – improving safety measures, changing the strategy, and changing the start point to Falcon Rock, just off Hout Bay and ending wherever we would find ourselves 24 hours later.

We didn't need to wait for a moon; I'd realized by now, from being out on the ocean at night, that I could paddle by feel, not by sight. I'd learned to 'see' with my other senses, by being in flow with the ocean – something I would master during the Atlantic crossing.

We called the event 36 hours out. We thought we had the right conditions. But at the last minute a tiny unforeseen low pressure weather system developed, so we decided to move the start further south and three hours earlier. I hoped that would put us ahead of the low pressure if it strengthened and moved in.

Sometimes you just have to take that leap of faith, put your head down, grit your teeth, start and hope for the best.

Everything started out amazing; absolutely blissful conditions with the sea like sheet glass, which made for the most incredible sunset on the water. There was not a breath of wind, just some of the most beautiful conditions I've ever paddled on the open ocean.

Things took a turn for the worse at about 8 pm, when that little low pressure strengthened and came into the coastline, exactly like we'd hoped it wouldn't. There was just no way of avoiding it. By 10 o'clock that night, the wind switched directions 180 degrees and we suddenly got headwinds and everything became instantly really bumpy, a very confused sea state, and basically went to shit in the space of an hour. Then a thick fog bank rolled in and made it suddenly really cold, with the wind and wet a compounding factor. Everything got so confused that I got seasick in the water. Oh, and I was circled by a shark!

Everything was just a mess and I was still trying to paddle. The north-wester was now howling and it was pitch black with no stars visible through the fog. Then the rubber-duck pontoons got a puncture, so my smaller safety support boat, tracking me just off the main support vessel, started sinking. After 10 hours and 23 minutes of paddling, the conditions were just way too dangerous and we had to call it off.

My biggest lesson from this second attempt was that we needed to find stable conditions and a more controlled environment. The only way we would be able to do that was to move the record attempt to where the ocean was milder, the water was warmer, and the wind was more constant. So instead of doing it on the cold Atlantic West Coast of South Africa, we decided to move the 24-hour record out of South Africa completely and up the east coast, to Mozambique. I was hoping for third time lucky.

■ ■ ■

Just over six months after the last two attempts, and with just under two weeks of the weather window left, I headed to Vilanculos, Mozambique.

The logistics for these kinds of missions are always immensely complicated, and even more so in another country. When I looked back on all the effort, training, planning, preparation, money and sacrifice that had gone into the last two attempts, with so much support from so many, I felt humbled.

Over the last year, I had been reminded numerous times that in order to succeed in the face of adversity and overcome the odds, it takes a team. But even more importantly, it's about resilience, self-belief, perseverance and dogged determination. I was ready for round three, and felt wiser, stronger and toughened by the wild elements of the Atlantic and the previous two attempts in the Cape of Storms.

'Testing the waters' is not just an expression. Knowledge only happens if you ask the right questions, *and listen*. I spent some time getting a feel for the ocean, how it all moves and breathes on the east side, with the help of some local fishermen, sailors and divers. I discovered some serious current and tidal movement I would need to work with, rather than fight against.

Stand-up paddleboarding for 24 hours straight is no joke. Being out in the ocean for 24 hours without stopping for more than a quick 15-minute hydration or nutrition top up was a massive undertaking. I knew now from past experience that the most difficult period was the six hours between 10 pm and 4 am, the graveyard shift.

But I pushed through to log 131 km in 24 hours, a new South African and All African Record. We saw a beautiful part of Africa, and were accompanied by dolphins, flying fish, and I saw my first ever dugong!

I'd now covered over 1270 km of solo missions, over three years, to fine-tune my hydration, nutrition, stamina and mindset, and prepare myself for any conditions that came my way. Getting through 24 hours in the open ocean was a big milestone for me mentally – now I knew I could do it. If I could pace myself properly, had everything that I needed to be completely self-sufficient, and could plan and manage my exposure to the elements there was no reason I couldn't go for as long as I needed to.

All I needed now was to design and build a craft, one that allowed me to get out of the sun and the elements between paddling sessions, was stable enough to right itself, could carry my water and my food, and hold its course when I wasn't on deck.

From that point, everything became about getting the funding to realize that dream.

But first, I had to hop on a plane to Molokai.

# Interlude: It's Not All About the SUP...

Lüderitz, Namibia | 26°39'48.12"S 15°9'20.83"E

Preparing for my cross-Atlantic solo expedition is the focus of this story, so I've concentrated on the preparation and the expeditions that helped me hone my skills, fitness, nutrition, my life-support and safety devices, and the design of my craft (more about that later).

But I wasn't just stand-up paddling over those five years. As a waterman, every watersport I do, be it sailing or surfing or stand-up paddleboarding teaches me something new about the ocean, and deepens my understanding of how to read the signs and make judgments that could mean the difference between success or epic fail – or even death.

So here are some of the things I was doing between SUP adventures. Let me say at the outset I was definitely doing too much. I learned the hard way about spreading myself too thin when I missed out on a really significant Big Wave event in Chile that could have had a significant impact on my life and brief big-wave surfing career, but hindsight is 20/20...

In June 2011 I was in France, competing in the Stand-up Paddleboard World Champs, while I was on standby for the premier Big Wave Paddle-in Surf Event in Chile, one of the last events on the Big Wave World Tour, which I was competing in at the same time as the SUP World Tour. It is an invitation-only event and can happen any time over a three-month window. It just so happened that when that event was called on (which means, it was going to run) 48 hrs later, I was in the SUP semi-finals. I knew it was going to be very tight making my flight, but I was sure I could pull it off. I opted out of the final and headed straight to the airport, but I didn't realize it was one of France's biggest national holidays, so the traffic was horrendous and flights all fully booked and no matter how I tried, I blew it! I couldn't get to the airport in time and missed the only two flight options that would get me to Chile in time for the event from France.

I didn't know it at the time, but because of my performance and win at Mavericks event in such big surf, my points for the tour were doubled and all I needed to do was to get through the first heat of the Chile event and I would have won the Big Wave World Tour Crown that year.

So, yeah, sometimes when we're juggling too many balls we drop some. I definitely learned a great lesson from that: don't spread yourself too thin!

Work out which balls in life you can juggle and drop, which will bounce, and which ones you make sure you never drop, as they will break and are irreparable.

In April 2014 I married my fair maiden, Clellind, in a small, rustic ceremony on a beautiful white sand beach in Langebaan. She is an amazing woman and we had a lot of great adventures and inspiring moments together. Our energies were good, and it was one of the most special times of my life.

In October, I was invited to compete in the Lüderitz Speed Challenge, in which top speed windsurfers from around the world fly in to see if they can break the world speed record. Basically it involves death-defying runs down a kilometer-long, four-meter-wide canal cut into the Namibian desert. You use narrow asymmetrical boards and weight jackets to help you go faster. I unleashed my inner speed freak and broke my own personal best of 46,7 kn or 85 km/hr! This was still far off the world record – and I was lucky not to break myself in a spectacular spinout at 85 km/hr on the final day!

In the end, the event wasn't about personal bests, pushing myself or evolving in the sport, but about the people who are part of it. I was reminded that it's not the destination that counts, but enjoying the people, the friendships and the magic moments through the journey.

In April I led the first ever stand-up paddleboard expedition through the Okavango Delta in Botswana. The mass of narrow, connected waterways are just teeming with wildlife, and it was an amazing way to grow both a love of stand-up paddleboarding, and a deep appreciation for some of the last, remote untouched African wilderness.

In 2015 we finally premiered my new film, *Ocean Driven*, about my epic quest to compete in the Mavericks Invitational, which I won in 2010. The film had taken three years to put together and had been well received. (It would go on to win five international awards.) Since we were going to be in California for the US premiere, we decided to add on a honeymoon to our trip. Clellind had always dreamed of going to Hawaii, and I was stoked to be able to show her this magical place of surfing legend that had been so much part of my big-wave journey. And because Clells was always super supportive of my expeditions and record attempts, she was also up for me competing in the Molokai while we were there.

We hopped on a plane to Honolulu just seven days after I completed the 24-hour record in Mozambique.

# Building the Dream (And Finding Some Money)

Cape Town, RSA | 33°55'43.29"S 18°25'14.43"E

After doing the 24-hour record and then the Molokai I felt I had a sense of the different conditions around the world. I knew that what I'd been dealing with in my training was next level compared to what I had seen anyone else doing, so I felt I was in a good place and space to take it to the next step.

I now held multiple world records and a Guinness World Record. I had pretty much tested myself in every single ocean condition and environment and I knew what I was going to have to deal with on the high seas. The 24-hour record, backed by the completion of the proof-of-concept paddle, solidified the idea that it was doable and now I knew, I was definitely going to do the crossing.

I was also clear that I wasn't going to have a support boat alongside me when I did it.

Once I figured that out, the next great challenge became building something I could be completely self-sufficient and independent in. If I could build a craft that could sustain me through all the conditions that I'd been out in over an extended period of time, then there'd be no reason why I couldn't do the crossing completely unsupported and unassisted.

I know a lot of people thought that that was absolutely insane and crazy but it was actually the greatest epiphany and light bulb moment. Once I got my head around the fact that having a support vessel was actually stopping the project going forward, all my efforts and all my thoughts went into building the right kind of SUP. I became obsessed with what it would look like, what length, what size, what weight, and who would build it.

I researched companies that had experience building similar craft, and could take everything I'd learned from the stand-up paddleboard side into what I wanted to build. It took a year to find the perfect people: Rannoch Adventures, UK-based boat building specialists in ocean-going rowboats.

Now I just needed to finance it.

I tried for three years to get the funding off the ground, and battled at every step of the way. I was on the verge of losing hope when, on the first of January 2016, while in Hawaii premiering *Ocean Driven* at the Waimea Film Festival, I got a mail requesting me to speak at a big corporate function in Johannesburg in South Africa in four days' time.

The company was called Carrick Wealth. It takes two-and-a-half days to get back to South Africa from Hawaii, but I told CEO Craig Featherby that I could pull it off – I could get a flight out on the 3rd to be on time to deliver a talk on the evening of the 5th, in SA. He was very concerned, rightfully so, on the timing; I would be flying 52 hours from the opposite side of the world to get there, and they would have over 1000 people gathered waiting to hear me speak. It was tight, but I believed it was possible. 'Well,' he said, 'if you can pull that off...'

'Trust me,' I told him, 'I've never been late for a talk in my entire life.'

The topic for the talk was 'Finding Courage', so I just had to do it. Having courage is the key to most magic and success in life, but you have to have the courage to try, to say yes, to take that first step, to start that first stroke...

I walked straight out of my film premiere into a taxi to the Big Island international airport, with 15 minutes to spare for the one and only flight that would get me to South Africa in time for the talk. After 52 hours flying and 4 connecting flights I arrived in Johannesburg where a taxi was waiting to take me to the conference venue. I had a shower, got into the tux I'd had delivered the day before, and walked into the venue with 15 minutes to spare. I delivered my talk on 'Finding Courage' and received a standing ovation.

Craig came up to congratulate me afterwards and asked me what project I was working on next. I told him, 'I plan to stand-up paddle, completely solo, unsupported and unassisted across the Atlantic, on a specialized craft to raise money for charity and ocean education.'

He said, 'No support, as in no supporting craft or crew?'

I said, 'Correct! When I rely on a support boat, with a support crew, there is too much that can go wrong, too much risk.'

'What kind of funding are you looking for?' he asked.

I told him how much. He asked me if I believed I could pull it off.

I didn't blink. 'I know I can! I can't really tell you why I know this, I just do… and when I tell you I'm going to do something like being here to deliver this talk today for your team, from across the other side of the world, I do. When I say I'm going to do something, I deliver, no matter what it takes!'

He smiled and said, 'Come back and speak to me on Monday. Let's see if we can make this happen.'

And that was the start of my relationship with Craig Featherby of Carrick Wealth, and the Transatlantic SUP Crossing.

# The *ImpiFish*

That's when the roller coaster really started. We wanted to launch the Transatlantic SUP Crossing at the end of that year. I believed with every fiber in my being in this project, and what it could achieve through the funds I would raise for The Lunchbox Fund and Operation Smile charities. But first, I needed to build my little craft.

I had half the funding to green light the project and start building with Rannoch.

I'd been working on the design for four years. It took three months to get contracts sorted, leaving six months to get the craft built and tested in England, and then shipped to Morocco to be ready to launch November 16.

The timeline didn't really seem realistic, but I knew this was my only chance and I had to do it, whether we found the other sponsors or not, even if I had to pay in the extra money myself – and we were talking serious money here.

By July 2016, we were already in the build phase, so I flew out to the UK to check on progress. Within hours of landing I was in Essex in a little factory shed in Burnham-on-Crouch, and all I could say was, 'Wow!' My vision was coming together right before my eyes! It was a truly pivotal moment. *Now you really are, all in! No turning back. Now you're going the distance, no matter what.*

My little unique board, just two feet longer than my normal open-ocean stand-up paddleboard was mid-stage in the build. There were three people buzzing around her, fitting struts and measuring the forward sleeping and navigation pod entrance for the main entry and exit hatch. The space was ready for the solar panels to be fitted on the back, and the outside of the pod would house the satellite communication and weather forecasting systems, the VHF radio, and autopilot system. There was just enough storage space for 50 liters of emergency water and freeze-dried food for 100 days. We were still waiting on the water desalinator and some emergency and safety gadgets, but it was real – it was actually real!

I decided to call her the *ImpiFish*.

I named her after the great Zulu warriors, the *Impis*, the most feared warriors in Africa, who were super tough and resilient, renowned for their courage and their fortitude, their strength and their perseverance. They would go the distance no matter the odds and the obstacles, they would never give up. So my *ImpiFish* was a warrior of the sea, and I needed to be *impi* warrior on the *ImpiFish* and find my own mental fortitude to go the distance, overcome the obstacles and the challenges and do the seemingly impossible.

People will make up every possible excuse not to do something, or give you a whole laundry list of the reasons why they 'can't'. You can always find plenty reasons if you look for them, but instead you should be finding reasons why you 'can'. Focus on *that* and then find a way to accomplish it. If you believe you can't you won't, but if you believe you can, and you want it badly enough, you will always find a way. It's that simple, period.

# Respect

At this time, a friend told me about a Frenchman by the name of Nicolas Jarossay, who was planning to stand-up paddle the Atlantic. At first I laughed – surely there couldn't be anyone else that nuts out there? But sure enough, a ballsy Frenchman was planning to paddle from the Cape Verde Islands, 1500 kilometers south of where I planned to leave from in Morocco, making his a way shorter route.

I was determined to leave from African soil, which is why I had chosen Morocco as my departure point, and decided to end my journey in Florida or the Caribbean. This meant that I could take advantage of the east-to-west trade winds. It also meant that my route would look like a smile across the Atlantic on a map: one of my main charities was Operation Smile, which provides life-changing surgeries for under-privileged children born with cleft palates.

But Jarossay had chosen the shortest possible distance across the Atlantic, from Cape Verde to Guadeloupe, which was a pretty smart call.

We went online and pulled up a picture of him paddling the craft he intended to do the crossing on. It took me about three seconds to turn to my friend and say, 'If you were to pay me a million dollars right now there is no way I would paddle that craft across the Atlantic.' He asked me why and I told him: It was super narrow and the freeboard above the water had no sides to be able to protect him at all; and the little companionway, where the hatch is to get in and out of his sleeping console, really didn't look safe or watertight, so if he turned over, that looked like it would take on water and if that happened, he'd be in a hell of a lot of trouble and he'd sink.

I did a little research and found he'd had to delay the start of his mission because he was having a problem finding a solution to have enough water onboard for his trip – which to my mind should have been the first obstacle to solve, at least six months to a year before you even think about the craft build. Water is the one key element to survival out there, so that's the first problem you solve.

I had a solar desalination system, a backup handheld emergency unit, and space for some backup emergency water. I had ensured that my craft's watertight compartments and hatches were rock solid; if it turned over, it was designed to self-right automatically. From his photo I could immediately tell that his board wouldn't do that easily, if at all.

Two weeks later, I learned that Jarossay had left from the Cape Verde Islands on 4 April, to start the 2950 mile journey. Unfortunately, he didn't even last 50 miles. One of his rudder lines snapped, he got turned sideways and was broadsided by a wave that flipped over his craft in pretty wild conditions; it took in water through its 'watertight' hatch and then didn't right itself.

Luckily he was only 50 miles offshore. He triggered his emergency beacon and mobilized Sea Rescue from Cape Verde. It took them an entire day to find him – they were calling off the rescue just after sunset and were on the way back to the harbor when they spotted Jarossay, in the dark, hanging on for dear life to the side of his upside-down craft, and hypothermic. He was in such a bad state that he passed out twice on the journey back to shore.

They tried to tow his craft back, but because it was so heavy, and the drag was draining their fuel, they had to cut it loose and let it go.

I was just glad he made it back in one piece.

The fact that he even started a project like that takes immense courage, and I have huge admiration and respect for him, as I know what it took for him just to get to the start line. The amount of time, energy, money and sacrifice that it takes to get to that day is enormous and very few will ever have any inkling of what a project of this scale requires. That's legendary already.

People often ask me what inspires me and my answer is always the same. I'm inspired by anyone who has the courage to follow their passions, goals and dreams and live their greatest life, no matter the odds stacked against them and how long it takes to achieve them. Whether they do or don't succeed makes no difference, as long as they try.

One of my favorite quotes is from 'The Man in the Arena', a speech by Teddy Roosevelt.

> 'It is not the critic who counts,' he says. 'The credit belongs to the man who is actually in the arena... who strives valiantly; who errs, who comes short again and again, because there is no effort without error and shortcoming... who spends himself in a worthy cause... who knows... the triumph of high achievement, and who at worst, if he fails, at least fails while daring greatly... his place shall never be with those cold and timid souls who know neither victory nor defeat.'

I'd rather die in the arena than be one of the negative whispering critics in the bar, who's never tried anything great, has never even had the courage to step into the arena to dare greatly. The greatest sin in life, I believe, is dying with regrets of all the things you wished you could have and should have done and tried, all those unfulfilled dreams.

At the same time, it made me very aware of the fact that Jarossay had just attempted a very similar voyage to the one I was planning – mine was just a third longer (by 1000 nautical miles, or NM). I was about to do a 4000 NM journey on a craft that was even smaller than his, at just over 19 feet long.

With my project and craft build in full swing by this point it just made me even more vigilant about quadruple checking everything and ensuring I had a backup of a backup of a backup. Often on these kinds of expeditions it's something small and simple that can scupper the entire project – and getting it wrong can end your life. So you absolutely do have to sweat the small stuff – a lot, in my case.

I was going over everything, again and again and again and again, to find any chink in my armor, anything that could unravel it all. I had to be so meticulous and obsessed with every detail. Nothing could be forgotten or unchecked, there had to be a backup of *everything*.

There were some fixes I needed to do to my own body, too, before I left.

# The Healing Power of Visualization

Kommetjie, RSA | 34°8'35.24"S 18°19'53.03"E

Once we were full green light with the project, my craft was in the build phase and everything was in motion, I went to go see Dr Steve Roche, the best shoulder surgeon in South Africa, probably one of the best in the world.

On 21 April he took some X-rays and he gave me the prognosis: 'Well Chris, you've been surfing, sailing and paddling for the last 40-odd years and you've damaged your rotator cuff from overuse. The only way you'll be able to get more use out of it is if we shave the actual rotator cuff – that can give you a little more longevity, and it'll stop your shoulder from wearing as badly, which is why you're getting the pain.'

I was going into this major project in five months. Was there enough time after the recovery period for me to do the training I needed before I left? He told me that it typically took four to six months.

I walked out of there worried. If the surgery didn't go as planned or the healing time took longer, it would jeopardize the project. But based on the amount of pain I was dealing with while training, I didn't think it was possible to do the project without it – I wasn't going to be able to paddle 4000-plus NM in my current state.

So for me it was a no-brainer: just focus on what you can control, namely the mental side and the healing. I was going to just have to amplify the visualization to improve healing and recovery on an exponential level. I had done it before with my knee in 2006 and I could do it again, I knew the drill.

So that's exactly what I did. I put every waking thought into visualizing my recovery and healing. I would also use the down time to catch up on all the logistics and the planning side of the project.

The following week I drove to the hospital, checked myself in, had the surgery and drove home the following day with my arm in a sling. Definitely not what the doctor prescribed, but hey, you have to push your body to heal!

Three days later I went for a walk up the mountain and five days after that I went for a quick swim. I was supposed be in a sling for a couple weeks, but I'm not so good at that stuff. I know myself and the pain I feel is my barometer and indicator.

For the next three to five weeks I focused every effort, every thought and every waking minute on healing and visualization, while eating and drinking the right things to support my body and immune system to heal, and taking the right multivitamins and supplements to support bone recovery.

I went for my first really mellow surf up the east coast nine days after surgery, two days after having my stitches out. Within six weeks I was up to 80% functioning, and was pretty much back to 95% when I went in to see Dr Roche for my two month check-up. He said it was the quickest shoulder surgery recovery he'd ever seen. He wasn't very happy to hear that I'd been surfing a week after the surgery, but he just laughed and said, 'Well, that is the power of the mind. You're a great example for other patients – I can tell them your story as a best-case scenario.'

I didn't mention that I was just about a paddle 4000 NM across the Atlantic – probably best to leave that small detail out!

# Bottleneck

In the last months before the crossing, I started to have challenges across pretty much every area in my life.

I don't think anybody quite understood the amount of stuff that I was trying to juggle. I was planning on doing something that no one had ever done before, and the pressure to get the craft right and my preparation right and the logistics right was immense.

I was running multiple businesses while also trying to get funding for the rest of the project, which was proving really challenging. Key decisions needed to be made daily while my craft was being built in the UK. There were all the logistical aspects of the project: funding; safety; electronics; backups; media; sponsorship obligations, team visas, project food, accommodation and flights… all the while simultaneously trying to train, build the team, keep my relationship together and make a living.

I was burning the candle on both ends and I look back on it now and it just seems crazy. It was just too much for one human to handle, and it took its toll – especially on my relationship with my wife.

Clellind and my separation was the toughest call I had to make through this all. I simply could not handle the stress that it was putting on me, on her, on us. I couldn't quite keep it together and I just couldn't give more than I was, which unfortunately, wasn't enough.

During this time we both realized that we wanted different things from life and that's okay. We both had so much love and respect for each other, that was never the issue, but sometimes, love alone is not enough. She's such an amazing human and I just wanted her to be happy, so if I wasn't able to do that and help give her that, then I knew it was best to let her find that special someone that could. Probably the hardest thing in my life was to let her go.

I was still working a full-time job trying to build a speaking business, and attemting to juggle my agency business with my assistant, who was taking over while I was building this project. I was still training, two to three hours a day, over and above that, while trying to get the craft finished in time, on budget, in another country, so I would still have time to test it, which was just a crazy feat in itself! I also had pretty serious weather window deadlines to ensure I was able to leave at the right time of the year, before the hurricanes started and it became too dangerous.

Everything just started to stack and bottleneck. It was the most crazy, stressful and challenging time in my life. There was also a lot of pressure from people who weren't supportive about my project. As I was battling through my relationship challenges I had some amazing close friends to lean on, but got little support from family which made it even more challenging for me. So I just isolated myself from anyone and everyone who was negative and just kept pushing forward.

Negative people don't serve you, ever, and especially when doing this kind of project. You want to surround yourself only with people that love, help, encourage and support you. Those who fan your flame rather than douse your fire.

Anybody that didn't contribute positively to the forward momentum of the project just literally got mentally and physically removed, like a cancer. It became that simple.

It got quite lonely, because there were so many doubters out there. It's easy to judge from a distance; a lot of people do, because it's easier to pass an opinion than step up and try anything of consequence yourself. Those people, the critics, are my worst; the ones who do nothing, but are happy to sit on the sidelines and point out faults or negative opinions, but have done nothing positive in life to help humanity or make the world a better place.

After Jarossay's attempt a lot of people had negative things to say about me going forward with my plan. The only person that didn't have any doubt was me! It just never crossed my mind that I couldn't pull it off. I just knew deep down inside that I could do it. Like I knew it with Mavericks, Jaws and the 12-hour record – some things I just know! It's that simple to me. I can't really explain it, it's like a deep certainty, a premonition. In my mind, it's already done.

The experience from the many journeys and adventures and all the sports I had done all my life had prepared me for exactly what I was working towards doing.

But I had no idea the sinister level of challenges I was about to face.

# Sabotage

The next three months were a blur. I was trying to keep it together, stay focused and positive, and roll with the seemingly never-ending punches until the day I could fly out to meet my little craft – my *ImpiFish* – that would be shipped to Morocco in late October.

The challenges just didn't stop. There was one seemingly impossible obstacle after another. Two sponsors pulled out at the last minute, due to financial constraints, which meant the project ran out of money. I got the money I was owed for *Ocean Driven* paid out to me in cash to add into the project. I re-mortgaged my house and put all I could afford on the line to fill the shortfall... but it still wasn't enough. I pulled everything I had, from every credit card, my mortgage account and my business overdraft, to make it happen.

I was still training six, sometimes seven days a week. I trained off Cape Point, in the wildest, most rugged sea and weather conditions on the planet, at least twice a week. I'd be out for up to six hours at a time, solo and unsupported, testing myself, getting my mind right, testing all my gear, safety equipment, food and backups.

My training mostly included upwind training, which meant strapping a whole lot of weight (up to 30 kg) and gear onto my board and then paddling upwind for two to three hours (which would normally be about 10 to 15 NM), from Simonstown to Cape Point and then turning around and doing a downwind back to where I'd set out from; this was my reward for the hard slog to the turning point. I would always be paddling solo one to three miles offshore, just getting used to all the different scenarios and putting a lot of extra weight, strain and load on my body.

I needed to get as comfortable as possible with being uncomfortable, putting my body and mind under as much load and strain as I could, to mimic any environment I was likely to encounter on my journey before it happened, so when it happened, it wasn't a surprise and I was already comfortable with it.

I tested different paddles, blade sizes, shaft lengths and flex patterns, to find a combination that would accommodate my body being under such load for long periods. I experimented with smaller blades, with more flex in the shaft, which would absorb a lot of the weight and strain and alleviate the huge amount of stress on my body, as well as slightly shorter shafts, to again reduce the load, when paddling into intense and strenuous conditions.

I spent a lot of time up the West Coast, at our little place in Langebaan, where I would focus on gear testing, flat-water training, and most importantly: the solo night training.

Most nights I would paddle with all my gear, up the lagoon for 5–10 NM (9–18 km), just to get a feel for paddling alone, in sheer blackness. My mind had to get used to not depending on sight, but rather adjusting my balance and feeling with my other senses. Slowly but surely I became more comfortable with being in an environment which most people fear: the ocean alone at night.

I didn't think much about it, or talk to anyone about it, I just got on and did it by myself, because I knew what I needed to do to mimic every scenario I would experience out there alone in the Atlantic Ocean.

Then, in the last two months before I was due to start my epic journey, a couple of weird things started happening. I've never been a paranoid person, but it was almost like someone was trying to derail the project, to purposefully stop it from going ahead.

I started to get a lot of random phone calls, with no one on the line, which I have never had before. I didn't really think anything of it, until one morning I reversed out of my driveway and heard a weird noise, super faint. My car was a Mitsubishi Pajero, 4X4, a really solid vehicle. I stopped to look around the car and couldn't see anything, but still something didn't sound right. Just before I turned on to the freeway into town I had a really uneasy feeling so I stopped to check again. I got right underneath the front of the car and saw nothing, and then I scooted around to the back and that's when I saw something strange: my rear axle looked like it had been cut and was almost about to separate.

I phoned JJ at the Mitsubishi dealership. I've known him for a long time and explained what I was seeing; he advised me to drive really slowly to the Mitsubishi dealership so he could take a look. He said he would put it up on a lift and call me with feedback. Two hours later he phoned and asked, 'Chris, are you sitting down, because there's something pretty serious I need to ask you… is there any chance anyone is trying to get rid of you, as in knock you off?'

He'd been working for Mitsubishi for 12 years and said that he'd never seen anything like it. 'The axle has been deliberately cut,' he said. 'You can see the marks of the hacksaw blade. And it's been purposefully cut down to the last small increment, to make sure that, when the vehicle was going around a corner with speed, under load, that it would sever and cause a major accident.' He had spoken to a couple of other Mitsubishi agents, and they had all come to the same conclusion.

It was like something out of a movie. I was still trying to get my head around it two days later when our cat Stitchy went missing. The next day I got a phone call from the vet to say they'd had an anonymous call – the person wouldn't leave their details, but told them to call me and let me know that my cat had been found at the side of the road. Our beloved Stitchy was dead.

I was still getting these random weird phone calls, with no one on the other side. The combination of all those things started making me really uncomfortable. I phoned David Becker, a good friend, sports lawyer and mental coach. We'd been working on some audio programs to help me through the crossing. He knew someone who had been a bodyguard for Nelson Mandela and now runs a protection service. He said he would speak to him and call me right back.

'Listen buddy,' he said less than an hour later. 'Someone is intentionally trying to stop you going forward with this project. So you're gonna need to pack up all your stuff and move out within the next six hours. Can you do that?' He'd arranged a place where I could stay. 'You must not disclose any information about your movements, whereabouts, flights, anything, to anyone, until you leave South Africa,' he said. 'We'll deal with Morocco when you are there.'

Obviously, this was a pretty major issue to deal with, over and above the stress of everything else happening, in my last week of being at home. It was also the last straw.

Packing up everything that I needed for the entire expedition would normally take a couple of days, but I had to do it within hours with an armed guard in a car waiting for me outside my house. I couldn't quite fathom what was actually happening, it was an intense situation to deal with before I left.

I moved out to a little hotel, was followed by the bodyguard, and basically couldn't tell anyone about my location in the final week leading up to my departure, and when or where I was going to be in Morocco. If I put something on social media, it should be opposite to what I was actually doing. These were pretty crazy times.

They would get even crazier. But there was something important I had to do first.

# Smile: Passion and Purpose

Bloemfontein, RSA | 15°58'4.17"N 23°58'28.81"W

Over the years I've become more and more mindful and aware of my impact, and that of my business, on the planet. I've always tried to focus on doing the right thing for the world, our oceans and others around me. You have to walk your talk in everything you do; let your actions define you.

For my business, that means adopting a mindful and sustainable ethos, and doing our best to offset any negative impact we have on our environment. For me personally it means being a positive role model and using what I do as a force for good.

My charity work is a big part of that ethos, and while I give a lot, it's something that gives me back far more than I ever bargained for.

A week before I was scheduled to fly out to Morocco, I travelled to Bloemfontein to witness lives being transformed. To celebrate their 10-year anniversary, Operation Smile planned to do 50 operations in in five days. Since I was raising money on the trip for Operation Smile, I wanted to see their work in real life. I wanted to be very clear in my purpose and witness first hand the kind of impact it had on the lives of children born with cleft palates, who could not otherwise afford surgery to correct it. When I planned the route of my crossing, I saw that it looked like a smile stretching across the Atlantic Ocean. I thought that was perfect.

By this point I had funneled my every last cent into the project – I literally had R8000 (less than $500) to my name, and I spent it on the flight up to Bloemfontein. My plan was to spend the day at the hospital observing the surgeons to really get a feel and sense of what I was doing this for, and how it was going to help these kids. It turned out to be a life-changing day.

When I arrived at the hospital at 6:30 am I saw lines of people lying on the ground outside the hospital gates. They had slept there overnight, with their children. Some of them didn't even have blankets to keep them warm. Many of the children seemed unfazed by their deformity, but the mothers understood the impact it would have on their lives; some of them had staked everything on getting this operation.

I spoke to some of the mothers who had spent three or four days walking, sleeping in shelters, doing whatever it took to get their child to that hospital that day, because they literally had nothing. I hadn't realized that until I spoke to some of the mothers and spent some time playing games with some of the kids before they went into surgery. That put a really powerful perspective on things.

It made me realize all the things we take for granted. You may think you don't have much, until you meet these parents who have no transport, no food, no money, and can't get their kids medical treatment. And they've spent days walking, doing whatever they can to get a little child to the hospital that day, because they know that the free operation, which is something that they'd never be able to afford, will literally change not only the child's life, but that family's life forever. It was a very humbling day.

Just being part of the surgery that day and watching those little faces getting transformed, seeing the raw emotion on a mother's face, the gratitude and happiness, was so powerful. It really clarified my purpose, knowing how my journey was going to have such a massive impact on so many little kids and their families' futures.

Even though it cost me everything I had left to go up there, it was probably the most important day of my preparation. With everything else going on, including someone literally trying to off me, this visit really brought things back into perspective. It gave me a very powerful understanding of why I was doing what I was doing. I was going to overcome whatever obstacle people threw my way to start this journey, get through to the other side, fulfill what I'd set out to do, and make it count. I was going to leave an inspiring legacy and change the lives of thousands of kids. No matter what, I was going the distance.

That day really helped me become very clear on a very powerful purpose – on my 'why' and to build a more resilient mindset to overcome and deal with all that was happening in my world. There is a wonderful piece by the great sage Patanjali that sums up what happens when you are truly inspired by something and have a sense of purpose. It goes like this:

> *When you are inspired by some great purpose, some extraordinary project, all your thoughts break their bonds: your mind transcends limitations, your consciousness expands in every direction, and you suddenly find yourself in a new and wonderful world that you never realized existed before. Dormant forces, faculties and talents that were never available to you before, suddenly come alive, and you find yourself to be a greater person by far than you ever imagined yourself to be.*

That's what happens when you are truly inspired by an incredible project, a purpose that is greater than yourself.

I left that day knowing that thinking about those kids would power me to get through literally anything.

# Breakdown to Break Through

Cape Town, RSA | 33°55'43.29"S 18°25'14.43"E

The week before leaving I had a farewell with about 20 close friends. Clellind was also there – even though we were separated, we were still super close and connected, cause she's such a special girl and superstar in spite of all we went through together.

I gave a short speech and I think it was the first time a lot of people grasped how much pressure I'd been under and the enormity of what I was actually going to do. My good friend Andrew stood up to speak and I think that the gravity hit him then; he couldn't assure everyone that I would be coming back in one piece, if at all. A lot of people in the room got quite emotional.

Later that evening, after a couple of drinks, I was talking to a friend and I broke down in tears trying to describe the financial pressure, the people trying to intimidate and kill me, having bodyguards and my cat being killed, and just the enormous amount of pressure and responsibility on me to do this project and go the distance. It was one of the toughest nights of my life in a lot of ways, but sometimes you need to move through hell, keep going and just let it all go. As much as I wanted to be in a really positive state before I left, that night was a necessary release.

Sometimes I think you have to break down to break free, to let out all that stress, to reboot, reset, to move forward stronger and refocused. It's like starting fresh, it's the calm after the storm, when everything's new again and it seemed a little easier to see the way ahead.

# Ready, Steady... What?

The final morning, I was packed and ready to set out early. After a final body realignment session with Dr John Thompson, I headed to the airport to meet Darren Robertson, my good friend, project financial officer, and support crew member through most of my projects. My film team and Clellind were also there to see me off.

It was a difficult goodbye at the airport, but by this point I was just so desperate to get on that plane and get out of there, away from all the madness in South Africa. I think I had already left days ago in my mind – now I just wanted to leave all the negativity and challenges behind.

I said farewell to my hometown through the airplane window. As the wheels lifted off the tarmac I leaned back into my seat and let out a huge sigh: I was finally away from it all, I was finally free.

Or so I thought.

After running through some final logistics, and trying to settle my mind with a film, I drifted off to sleep and woke an hour before landing in Dubai to catch my flight to Morocco.

I only had 45 minutes to transfer. As I was crossing between terminals, I connected to the wifi. That's when the message came through on my phone. It was from Darren. *Hey, bud, just double-checking that you want me to transfer the 20,000 pounds to that new account in the UK?* I sent a quick message back to him: *Ha, funny one brother. Good joke! I don't know what you're on about! Anyway, catch up on the other side.*

Two minutes later, I get a message back from Darren saying, *What are you talking about? I received your mail, with the urgent payment instructions and I'm just double-checking, before I transfer the money. You are kidding that you didn't send it, right?*

I was trying to get to my next flight before the gate closed. I told him I had no idea what he was talking about. *Jumping on a flight. Let's sort it out on the other side? I haven't sent any emails to you in the last 12 hours as I've been on the flight.*

A couple of minutes later, I get an SMS back saying he'd just forwarded the mail I'd supposedly sent him. *Are you joking, because I'm getting gray hairs dealing with this shit!*

I sent a quick response asking him not to transfer any money under any circumstance until we talked on the other side. *As you know we're pretty much broke with the project and that last 25K is all accounted for...*

I went into my emails while I was boarding and sure enough I see a perfectly constructed email sent from my account, to Darren, sent five minutes after my flight took off from Cape Town for Dubai. WTF?

The mail was exactly as I would have written it, using exactly my wording and terminology: '*Hey Darren, just about to fly out and just got an urgent request from the Rannoch guys in UK building the craft requested that last bit of money to be paid, regarding to all the other bits and pieces that we needed last minute, please can you send it as a matter of urgency, before I get to the other side, attached is the invoice. It's all been approved. Please can you get it sorted, so it's paid before I arrive on the other side, as they are stressing.*

*Thanks, bud. Really appreciate it. Chris.*'

It was like someone had been watching and monitoring my account and tracking every mail, so they knew exactly how to make it sound just like me.

It was the most perfectly constructed fraudulent effort. They knew all the details, including my flights, what time I was leaving and when I was going to arrive, so they could get it paid after I took off and the money transferred before I landed in Dubai.

It was literally the last money that we had in our account, intended for everything outstanding over the next month in Morocco, including satellite communications data, my forecaster, flights, Airbnb and living expenses for myself and the team.

If I hadn't seen the email myself, I wouldn't have believed it was even possible. It was as if someone was doing all they could to stop me going forward with the project. It was just never ending – one weird and crazy thing after another.

Once we arrived in Morocco, things should have been a whole lot easier. But it wasn't over yet.

The *ImpiFish* had vanished.

I spent the first week in Morocco trying to track down my little craft. It was supposed to arrive at the same time as me, but it had just disappeared. I had the full shipping manifest and a detailed shipping itinerary of the craft, and it was meant to be in Agadir. It seemed my little *ImpiFish* was sent to the wrong country, then put on a ship and sent to Casablanca, also the wrong location, 12 hours north, which shouldn't have been possible, as the shipping manifest didn't show that on the itinerary at all.

Nic Maunder, an old sailing friend, jumped in to help with the logistics; we had to get my craft as a priority, and also find the two pallets of gear that had mysteriously been delayed in a shipment from South Africa, which no one could explain.

Two weeks after it was meant to land in Agadir, my craft finally arrived. I'm not a suspicious person, but that never happens when the details are all clear on the bill of lading and the ship's manifest. If both myself and my team weren't following up on every detail, every second of the day, we wouldn't have got the craft for another two weeks – which would have put us out another month, late for the project start and into hurricane season.

We spent two full days in customs trying to get the SUP released from dock officials – to no avail. No matter what paperwork we showed them, they wanted something else. Eventually we hired a local Moroccan import agent to help us negotiate with customs and get any additional paperwork sorted, just so we could get the container opened and get the craft out and in the water!

*It's all part of the journey and the adventure. Follow the process, follow the process. Eye on the prize, I reminded myself mentally. Breathe, slow it all down, roll with it. It's Morocco, we will get there... breathe, breathe!*

That afternoon, after almost five days going back and forth and paying a little to one official here, a lot to another one there, and bouncing between the same five offices and the port control offices in the harbor in the blistering heat five times in the same day, we finally got the paperwork stamped, got the craft out of customs, out of the container and to the Agadir Marina.

What a relief, just getting my little craft lowered into the water. It really was a monumental moment. It was a tight drop-in launch spot, as we weren't allowed to use the slipway; if I wasn't so focused on not letting her get damaged as she was being craned into the water, I would have been a lot more emotional!

That evening Nic and I went to dinner to celebrate the craft being in the water and our shipment of gear being in the air, on the way to us.

As we were toasting with our second beer, he lowered his tone and said 'Hey, I was waiting for the right moment... I didn't want to talk to you about this until we got the craft in the water, but we have run into a bit of a problem in South Africa with all the food for the project.'

We had meticulously chosen and planned out all the nutrition and freeze-dried food for the expedition over the last three months. Everything was sorted and sponsored; we had 15 different meal recipes picked out to be carefully packed into daily rations for the journey.

Nic said, 'Remember the challenge you were having collecting the sponsored freeze-dried food after it was all confirmed? Remember I said I would arrange to collect it from them over the next couple of days, and you mentioned they seemed a little off about the collection?'

The dinner we'd just shared was starting to turn in my stomach.

'Well,' Nic said, 'I don't really know how else to put it, but the company has gone bankrupt!'

So we were not getting any of that food.

'Don't freak out, but we're looking at alternatives. The guys are on it back in Cape Town and said they've found some stuff and don't want you to stress about it. They're going to send you whatever they can find in the next week.'

I didn't really know how to respond. Obviously this stuff is pretty specialized – we'd picked out every meal pack for the exact number of days, with different choices and nutritional values. Now we were scrambling around trying to find one of the most important elements of the entire project. If we didn't get that right, it could be the downfall of the entire crossing.

The food nightmare didn't end. I only realized when we were packing the food into the craft that there were only three different types of freeze-dried food packs, rather than the 15 different choices I'd made to last over the 90-odd days and ensure that I had balanced nutrition. Instead, I got Nasi Goreng, Ham and Leek, and a Carbonara. That is what I would be eating every day, every meal, for the next 90 days, and pretty much nothing else.

That might not sound like much of a big deal or a challenge to you, but when you're eating the same three items every day for over three months, your body will start revolting. I knew there was going to be an issue going forward, but at that point there was literally nothing I could do about it.

I'd spent months making sure one of the most important aspects of the project was taken care of. Your food and your key nutrition planning for expeditions like this can be the difference between success, failure and major health issues. So this was a massive challenge to get my head around.

# Staying on Course

Essaouira, Morocco | 31°30'31.92"N 9°45'54.86"W

Every day there seemed to be a new mountain of obstacles to overcome in Morocco, but we worked our way around them and through them, day in and day out, while making new friends along the way.

While I was waiting for the rest of the team to arrive, I drove up to a place called Essaouira, which is three hours to the north of Agadir, and sticks out at the top of the bulge of Morocco. It would be an easier place to leave from, because once I got past the first two miles off shore I would be totally clear for the rest of the Moroccan coastline going forward, but the safety and logistics of that harbor were not ideal, so we decided to leave from Agadir – which meant that the weather window literally had to be perfect.

This in itself started becoming an enormous challenge, because the weather wasn't playing in our favor at all. If I left on the wrong day, I could get blown back onto land. It's a pretty dangerous coastline down there, and I needed at least a two-day weather window to get a safe 60 NM offshore; that window wasn't opening up at all, which started to become a huge concern.

Once I left the harbor I would not only need to get 60NM offshore to build a buffer away from land but also paddle another 350 km SW, before navigating my way through or around the Canary Islands, and making my way south and west to pick up the trades. I planned it this way, so that if anything went dramatically wrong in the first two weeks, I would have the option of coming in to the Canaries to do emergency repairs.

Looking back, I realize that was just wishful thinking – but I'm

Since I was going to be alone at sea for at least 90 days, I needed failsafe communications and navigational equipment. If you are a sailor you can skip this next part, but if you aren't familiar with boats it might be interesting to know what I had on board my little *ImpiFish*.

- VHF (Very High Frequency) radio: this allows you to communicate offshore when there is no solid signal available. Its frequency is generally line-of-sight, which at sea is roughly 20 miles (30 km). The very high frequency band allows you to communicate from ship to ship or ship to shore, if you are in range. Channel 16 is the emergency channel, which all vessels should monitor 24/7 to pick up distress signals. If you send a mayday call, any ship or yacht in a 20-mile radius around you should be able to hear you and respond. But if you are in the open ocean and you don't have any vessels or ships or yachts in close proximity – which is very normal – the likelihood of anyone hearing you is very slim. I believe that every vessel should have at least one VHF radio on board. I always have at least one main one in my craft, and two more: one in my emergency grab bag which will go with me into the tiny Life raft if I get into trouble, and one that I carry with me on deck so I can communicate with ships without having to go down into my cabin.
- GPS (Global Positioning System) gives you your exact position – latitude and longitude – anywhere on the planet using satellite location. Most GPS will allow you to put in a waypoint, which is a point on a chart you can navigate towards. The GPS will give you your location relative to the waypoint. I always have multiple GPSs on board, one in the grab bag for emergency.
- The chartplotter is a bigger unit with a display, which links to my GPS unit. That means that you can chart your course, your direction of travel, and your routing. It is the best method of routing because you can put in your waypoint and see exactly where you're going, what the distances are, your current speed and roughly how long it will take you to get there.

- AIS (Automatic Identification System) enables you to program data like your GPS into your chartplotter; it will then give you all the different vessels and ships in the area so you can see where they are relative to yourself and take evasive action if necessary. Your AIS can also be linked into your MMSI number (Maritime Mobile Service Identity), which will allow you to give your information – what kind of vessel you are, your size, your last location and your destination – to surrounding ships. This allows them, and you, to determine vectors and angles regarding how long it's going to take them to get to you so you don't get run over. It's a very, very important piece of kit, especially if you don't have radar.
- The Echomax is like radar. When a ship sends out a radar signal it hits the Echomax and is reflected back at the ship; it will then make one come up on their radar telling them you are there. When the craft sends out that radar signal, which is happening all the time, it deflects off the ship and gives a little beep on my side so I know we've been picked up by something within a 10-mile radius. The closer that vessel gets to me, the louder and more frequently the Echomax beeps.
- EPIRB (Emergency Position Indicating Radio Beacon) is the last resort for emergencies or when you are in imminent danger. When you pull a pin on the EPIRB it sends out an electronic positioning signal via satellite to the emergency services that monitor and manage distress signals around the world. They have the info registered to your craft so they know the size, the shape, who it belongs to and the emergency contact details. Once they receive the signal they contact the closest vessels that can assist; they are bound by maritime law to respond once they get notified that there's a craft in distress. So it is another very important piece of kit.
- PLB (Personal Locator Beacon) – These are integrated into your GPS now; a great one is the Garmin inReach Explorer, which is a PLB, GPS and satellite texting communication device all in one. Probably the most functional device you could have as an emergency backup to your main systems.

- The Emergency Strobe, which I called the Firefly, is a powerful strobe light that makes it easy to be spotted from a distance. It's normally a white light, which flashes regularly for 6 to 12 hours. Generally you want to attach it at the highest point on the craft so it can be seen relatively easily.
- BGAN Explorer Extreme is my main satellite communication unit for sending messages and updates once out of cellular range from land, which is generally about 5–10 km offshore. It didn't always work and needed decent weather, little movement and to be pointed directly at the closest satellite all the time, which was incredibly challenging on a craft as small and volatile as the *ImpiFish*.
- ISAT Phone 2 – A satellite phone that worked intermittently, but also generally only when conditions were mild and good.
- Katadyn Power Survivor 40 Watermaker – The smallest and best 12 volt water-desalination unit available for boats of any size. It sucks in seawater from the sea and removes salt from the water via reverse osmosis, giving you fresh water to drink.

Of course all of these things depend on power, so I needed to make sure I could keep the batteries charged at all times. Which would prove to be one of my biggest challenges.

They were also all critically important because for much of the first part of my journey I would be traveling through the shipping lanes. Roughly five miles in width, these are where large vessels or super-tankers travel. Areas where there is a lot of marine traffic can be extremely dangerous for small vessels like myself because firstly, they can't see me, and secondly, they are so large they cannot easily turn or take evasive action if you are in their way. For this reason you are supposed to always cross them at 90 degrees, so you enter and exit them as quickly as possible. But you can only do this if you move very quickly, have working steering and have favorable wind direction and weather to maneuver out of them. For a 48-hour period, in the middle of the shipping lanes, I would have none of these things.

The terror of being at sea with 15 or 20 supertankers bearing down on you is second to none.

In terms of steering, besides my paddle, I had a rudder, which was connected to an autopilot (or autohelm) most of the time and for when I needed to take a break – break being the operative word, because that's what it did for most of my journey. But more on that later.

If I needed to rest or sleep, or if the weather was dragging me in the wrong direction, I could deploy either the drogue or para-anchor to slow me down. The parachute anchor attaches to the front of your craft (the bow) via a long line. (Not to be confused with a drogue, which is generally used off the stern.) Another line goes to the top of the parachute anchor; this is your retrieval line, which collapses the front of the parachute when you need to pull it back in.

Deployed off the side of your craft, it can either slow you down when you're going the wrong direction or stabilize the craft in heavy weather, or a combination of the two. I used the parachute anchor far more than I was meant to – especially when my autopilot failed, which was most of the time – to stop me going backwards or in the wrong direction when I had the wind against me. The parachute anchor is one of the most valuable tools on these kinds of expeditions, especially if you are solo.

Like any good sailor I also always would have multiple knives. I'll have two main knives up on deck, always with one side very sharp and the other side serrated so it makes it easier to cut through lines and ropes. A Leatherman or Skeletool multi-tool is also very important and comes in handy ALL the time.

In my toolbox I always have two rolls of duct tape and lots of electrical tape – between those two you should be able to fix a lot of stuff. I will try and get some gorilla tape for my next trip, to help seal leaks and plug holes. Expanding foam and emergency epoxy putty is an essential because it sets very quickly – and you can use it underwater, which is pretty amazing and also very useful in tight situations. Other than that I had a small hammer and two or three screwdrivers. I had a spanner and a shifting spanner, a small socket set, and a whole lot of fuses in a fuse kit. It's a very small kit, but has a torch and wire ties, some extra small bits, extra rope, lines and more trusty sail repair kit, darning needle and twine, a bungee cord, a thin rope and scissors.

# Leven the Incredible

As a sailor or ocean adventurer weather is either your best friend or your worst enemy.

As the end of November grew near, the weather was not playing nice in Agadir. Morocco was experiencing some of its angriest storms in more than 50 years, with winds up to 90 kn, or 103 miles (166 km) per hour. The latest storm had already dismasted a couple of big yachts, but we were hoping this Atlantic weather system would dissipate over the following week.

There was absolutely no way I could leave before it did.

It was already the 20th of November, and my visa was a week away from expiring. We had been in Morocco for more than a month, which was the longest period I could get a visa for. Now the authorities wanted me to fly back to South Africa to renew it.

I went back and forth to the visa office and consulate general in Agadir for three days trying to get an extension. They said they could extend my visa for an extra 10 days, but if I didn't leave the country before it expired, they would put me in jail. Not the ideal situation or circumstances to start my crossing under. If the weather didn't look right I would still be forced to start within 10 days, even though the stakes of leaving at the wrong time were life-threatening.

Without the knowledge of locals and making local connections, you are nowhere. Without the help of a local in Agadir called Mustafa, we wouldn't have even got the basic extension. Like most places in life… if you want to go quick go alone, if you want to go far, make friends and build a great team.

Over the last year, I'd built a small but great team behind me to help me make this project come to life. This gave me the confidence to know that when I pushed off that dock and headed out into the deep blue, everything had been taken care of and every box had been ticked.

One person can make all the difference between failure or success. I had been struggling to get one of the craft builders to fly over to run through everything with me and double-check all the systems in the 10 days prior to starting. I was running out of time, but had a backup plan. I had been put in contact with another very experienced ocean rower and sailing skipper, a fine gentleman by the name of Leven Brown.

So I called Leven, and said can you help? In his broad Scottish accent he said, 'Book me the flight and I'll be there in a flash!'

Two days later, Leven was there and it was the best decision of the entire project to fly him in so we could run through literally EVERY-THING together.

The only way to describe Leven is, incredible! He's a Scottish sailor and just a special human in every way – besides being one of the most knowledgeable, competent and experienced ocean rowers on the planet, who holds multiple ocean crossing world records. He understood the ocean and the weather and how to read them, just like me, only better. He had a calm, no-nonsense way about him that would see me through many a tough moment during the crossing, although I didn't know that at this point. I was privileged to have him on my team and I can't envisage having done this crossing without him. It all started with him coming to help me in Morocco.

Leven and I spent the next four days triple checking every single system, all the electronics, the batteries, the solar system, the drogues and drogue lines, the parachute anchor lines and bridles. When we started going through the watermaker, which is connected up to the solar and the backup mini manual, hand-powered watermaker (the same as the Marines use for their special ops) we discovered we'd been sent a sec-ondhand one – and it was damaged. I was pretty pissed off about that, because I paid for a brand new one, and if the main watermaker had broken down and I was relying on that backup, it could have ended my life. But you move forward; we got another membrane to replace the one that was split and fixed it. Letting go is the hardest thing to do, when errors have grave consequences, but holding grudges doesn't help get the job done, so let it go and move forward.

While we were testing all the systems with both of us on board the *ImpiFish*, one of us moved to the one side and we came very close to capsizing. It made me realize how vulnerable my little craft was and how easy it is to turn over. And that was a bit of a concern, because all it takes is one wave for the little craft to capsize or the hatch to be open and all your electronics and your entire project is pretty much done. Game over!

I didn't know it, but Leven would prove to be a steadying influence for me all the way across the Atlantic Ocean.

# The Waiting Game

Agadir, Morocco | 30°17'25.07"N 9°47'10.73"W

By the beginning of December we ran out of money. We had now been in Morocco three weeks longer than we'd planned and budgeted for. The project was over-extended across all levels; I had run through all my personal reserves and my business reserves too.

Now we were just waiting and praying for the weather to come right over the next week before my visa extension ran out.

All the project credit cards, as well as my personal credit cards I was using to pay for everything including the Airbnb, started to be declined everywhere. The three team members who were there with me – my photographer Alan van Gysen, Darren, my film guy Adrian Charles and Leven – all flew out, leaving me very much alone.

It was around then that I also realized that it was essential to have Leven on the team for the rest of the project to do the weather routing and updates, and to run through everything when I ran into potential problems. But there was not a cent left to pay him to do that role. I had to figure out how I could find additional cash. The only option I had was that I was still owed money from my film *Ocean Driven*, which was still in the process of being sold to distributors. I made an agreement with the director that if she could pay me 50% of my fee upfront now, in cash, then I would forfeit the rest. So that's what I did – and thank goodness.

Like always, whatever it takes, if you want anything badly enough, you will always find a way.

That was hands down the best decision of the entire project, right there. I needed to have Leven as my long-distance backup, support and weather guy on this journey if I was going to stay alive. It was that simple.

As soon as everyone left, the weather window for the last day of my visa expiration, the 6th of December, started to look a lot better for departure! What were the chances of that happening? A million to one. I reckon I was due a little break. I had to hope, pray, meditate, visualize, whatever it took. I only had one chance to do this, and I had to get it right!

I spent the final day of preparations making a backup para-anchor and a backup drogue, and re-sealing all hatches for extra safety, after I discovered – much to my horror – a minor leak. At least I found it and was able to repair it pretty easily.

I changed out to a longer centerboard to reduce the leeway and cross track error (slipping sideways in the water). I repacked everything to get the balance and weight ratios and distribution right and repacked all the key essentials, so I'd have them all at quick access for the first key 48 hours – the para-anchor, drogue, and all lines, just in case I got pushed back onto land, which was my greatest worry.

I charged all the battery banks and backup battery units to full. Re-checked all solar charging units. Synched all communication devices to the satellite navigational systems, checked the tracker system and GPS systems and backups of both of those, checked the AIS was working correctly, all three VHFs, both the handheld ones and the main craft radio, and synched my music across all three devices.

Leven was sending me forecast updates on the weather every six hours and the first 3-day forecast was starting to look possible! We made minor tweaks to routing, timing, distances and buffer estimates, before we could make the final call on exact departure date and time. It was looking like 4 am or 5 am, on the 5th or 6th December, the exact day my visa was going to run out.

I double- and triple-checked all the systems again, cleaned the rudder and the bottom of the craft. I spent half a day at the main police station HQ arranging permissions and papers to leave. It can take a couple days to do this and once you do all the paperwork, you leave them with your passport, which is scary and you just trust and wait for them, sometimes up to two days, before they give you clearance to leave and your passport and documents back.

I have a rule I try and live by: when you're on your way out, always leave big smiles and happy hearts behind. So after one last final run through of everything, I headed an hour up the coast to give back a little to the community that had helped me here over the last four weeks.

I jumped in the water and surfed at the famous Anchor Point, and then gave my wetsuit, boards, board bags and some of my expedition shirts and gear to stoked friends and local kids I had met along the way, before heading back to town to wrap up any loose details.

This was to be my last night in a comfy warm bed on land for 90–100 days! I wanted to savor it, as in the morning I was moving my last two little bags onto the *ImpiFish*, my home for the foreseeable future.

The cabin is so small, when I'm lying down, my shoulders touch each side of the hull, side to side, and when I sit up in the cabin the hair on my head touches the roof, so it's a tiny space to work/relax/cook/live and sleep in. When I tried to sleep, my feet pushed up against the end of the pod, so I wasn't able to sleep fully stretched out either, my legs were always bent, it was that small!

I needed to make the inside of my survival pod as homely as possible. I try to surround myself with things that inspire, empower me and make me smile. So I had Squirt, a little stuffed turtle from Maryke Musson and the team at the Two Oceans Aquarium in Cape Town, where I do work with the turtle rehab, tag and release program, because I was racing a virtual turtle across the Atlantic. I also had a picture of some of the Operation Smile kids and one of me with one of the doctors from that really important day just before I left, to remind me of my purpose. I had a picture of my house in Kommetjie, a picture of Clells and me, and a picture of Stitchy our cat – even though she wasn't with us any more it still made me feel happy every time I looked at her picture.

I had a little travel guitar too – although in the end I wouldn't be able to play it because my fingers would split so badly from the salt water. And I had three little sponsored tot-sized bottles of Ardbeg whisky in a soft case to paddle across the ocean. One was for me to drink on New Year's Eve, weather permitting. One was for me to auction at the end of my trip for charity, and the last one would go back to them to commemorate my voyage.

I went back to the police customs and immigration office again, to get feedback on clearance. As we know, the squeaky wheel gets the grease.

I pre-mixed 18 liters (36-hours' worth) of Enduren hydration mix and kept it on ice while on land – there would be no fridge out there, but this way I wouldn't have to run the watermaker for the first 24 hours, which would save the full batteries for as long as possible. The first couple days weather looked like it was going to be overcast, which is not good for solar and charging, so I needed to be super careful. I also ordered two days' worth of sandwiches/baguettes to be delivered the night before I left, and had all my race food packed strategically on deck for quick access and availability.

The final countdown clock was running. T-Minus 12 hours and counting. I went through my final checklist.

Final weather updates and updated routing again – check. Mount the EPIRB in its special bracket outside on deck (always the final thing to do before you set off on any ocean voyage) – check.

PLB charged in the emergency grab bag, with all the other backup food and emergency gear, for quick emergency departure into my mini life-raft – check.

Satellite navigational systems synching to all devices – check.

AIS picking up all the ships in the 10-mile range and giving me their info – check.

Tweak the routing for the waypoints set in the GPS and chartplotter, according to the updates forecast – check.

Tracker working and reading – check.

GPS and backup units working – check.

VHF radio and backup unit receiving with a confirmation from port control that they can read me loud and clear – check!

All safety systems and lines in place – check.

All backup micro systems working – check!

Re-balance of the weight on my little craft so she's sitting level in the water for speed and glide – check, and we are ready to rock and roll. *Let's do this!*

As I enjoyed my last sunset on land for a long while, I thought that many would say I was about to start, but they would be so wrong. I'd already succeeded. The moment I pushed off that dock and took that first stroke, I will have achieved my goal. I had an idea, a vision, a dream and had finally brought it into reality. I was living what I believe and preach, which is always have the courage to follow your passions and know that it's never too late to live your dreams.

My brother Conn called to wish me *bon voyage*. He reminded me that I would take around two-million paddle strokes over the next 80–100 days. I reminded him that every stroke I took would fill lunch-boxes and put new smiles on thousands of children's faces over the next two years. I would be paddling a smile across the Atlantic Ocean.

Whatever it takes, for as long as it takes…

I was good to go. Game on!

# Slipping Out Quietly

Atlantic Ocean | 30°17'25.07"N 9°47'10.73"W

The final midnight weather update on December 5 sent a chill down my spine.

The weather had shifted again, and not in my favor. I would be paddling into a headwind – exactly what you don't want when you start out. It would be really light at first, gaining strength in the afternoon, so I guess that was a silver lining.

I believed I could punch out through it, if I started super early. So I brought my departure time forward to just after 4 am. *It is what it is, I told myself. It's never going to be perfect and if you wait for perfect, you will most likely never ever begin, so just start. Here we go!*

I was ready to cross the Atlantic, solo and completely unsupported and very much alone, on my purpose built, one of a kind, stand-up paddleboard.

Now I was just focusing, visualizing, resting and readying my mind for what was to come. I'd been mentally and physically ready for months. Actually, I'd been readying myself for this adventure for most of my life. Now I just wanted to get out there.

I focused on breathing deeply, visualizing what I wanted the outcome to be and how I was going to get through the next 48 hours, working through everything mentally, while I slowly and methodically taped each one of the fingers on my hands. I used special zinc oxide tape to help prevent and absorb the blisters that would follow over the next 48 hours – that was one thing of which I could be certain.

Because no matter how much training I had done, nothing was really going to prepare me for the first 48 hours. I was going to have to paddle my fully laden, almost 1-ton craft out more than 50 miles into a light headwind, solo for two days and two nights straight, with minimal sleep, in order to get me far enough offshore to build the buffer I needed. That light onshore breeze would mean that every moment I stopped paddling or was taking a break between sessions, eating or drinking or resting, I would be going backwards. After that the wind was due to swing more NE, then SE and then I could get a decent two or three hours' sleep.

I would probably need to paddle 15–20 hours per day/night so I didn't get blown back onto land. Getting blown onto the cliff-riddled coastline further south, down the Moroccan coastline, where there would be no help, no support, and no one to rescue me if shit went sideways, was my greatest fear.

Since my whole team had flown out a week ago, I was very much alone in this foreign country and I was about to leave off the dock at 4 am in the pitch black into the Atlantic Ocean to do something no human had ever done before. Never before have I felt that alone and vulnerable.

My goal was very focused and specific: survive the first 48 hours in one piece and build enough sea room between myself and land; if I could do that, then I would be able to get across the Atlantic. That's how simple it was for me at the start!

*Bite-size chunks, just break it down into bite-size chunks.* I could manage and focus on accomplishing that. Getting across the ocean wasn't the worry for me, because if I couldn't get out past that first 50 miles and build in the sea room needed, the project would be over. So I just had to focus on what was in front of me, focus on what I could control, make it happen and make it count.

I knew these first two days were probably going to be the toughest of the entire trip, so my sole objective, from the time I pushed off the dock was very simple: don't get shipwrecked down the coast of Morocco alone!

*There are going to be no second chances. So do it once, do it right, make the right choices right from the outset, give it all you got, and then*

*everything else you have in you, because that's what it's going to take –*
*everything you got and more.*

I also knew that no matter what my body was going to tell me, I was just not going to listen. It was going to be purely mental; override any messages about pain and fatigue... be mindful and clever, monitor, manage and pace the hydration, nutrition and tiredness, but never, ever give up!

All I needed now was get one night's decent sleep before it all began. At 10:30 pm I turned the lights out in my little *ImpiFish*, and drifted off to sleep.

Not 30 minutes later I heard talking outside and then BANG-BANG-BANG on the outside of the craft. 'Hello, this is Customs... can you open up sir?'

They needed me to sign two more documents. Even though I had lodged all the paperwork with them two days ago.

'Sorry guys,' I told them. 'I have my passport stamped, and I leave in five hours. Did you bring them to sign?'

'No, you must come sign!'

I told them in no uncertain terms that I was not about to leave my craft. 'Either you bring these documents here, please, or I must leave without signing them... I'm not going anywhere, I need to sleep!'

They said they would come back.

At 11:45 pm there was another bang-bang-bang on the side of the craft. I signed the documents, fumbling the pen with my taped hands. I don't even remember what they were for, I was so irritated, frustrated and tired by this point.

'Good luck!' they called, as they disappeared into the night. It was now just before midnight, and my alarm was set for 4 am, so I could be gone by 4:15 am. Great – four hours sleep before the biggest adventure of my life!

# The Start

When my alarm went off at 4 am I sat bolt upright.

I crawled out of my little cabin hatch and grabbed my little Jetboil stove, gas on, burner primed, flame ignition, the coffee press already prepped last night – we are game on!

I turned on all my systems and electronics, running through the checklist like a pilot checking instruments before take off – navigation lights, AIS, Echomax, GPS, chartplotter, battery charging unit, solar charged to 95%, VHF radio, instruments and repeaters on deck. Wind and GPS heading and waypoints reading, satellite nav and sat phone, on and charged.

I poured my coffee into my pre-prepped thermos cup with a lid, took a big swig, and moved from a crouch in the entrance of my tiny cabin with its soft red light into the brisk pitch black of the outside morning at 4:15 am.

It was dead calm, the water like sheet glass. This was good, the light onshore predicted hadn't started yet and maybe I could get two to three miles out before it all changed from these perfect conditions.

I took another big swig of coffee, looked down at my taped hands, breathed in deeply and then a long exhale out. I remember saying, *I need to go, I need to go right now!*

I crawled back into my cabin, changed into my gear ready for action, harness on, fleece top and beanie… *Let's do this!*

I put my 'Crossing Mix' on my iPhone, blue-toothed it to my outside speakers – set super low so only I could hear it. I stepped up onto the dock, unhooked the stern line, then walked forward and unhooked the bowline and threw it onto the deck of my little craft. Then I stepped back onto the *ImpiFish* with only the spring line connecting me to the dock, in the misty pitch black of the pre-dawn.

I stood there for a last few seconds, which seemed to last a lifetime, before I flicked that last spring line off from the bollard. I disconnected my new Ke Nalu paddle from its holding place up on deck, put my foot out against the dock to gently push the bow of the *ImpiFish* free… I breathed out, knowing what I was doing and said softly under my breath, *Just start! Don't think, don't hesitate, just start!*

It might be the last time I touch land for a very long time… or ever.

It all felt pretty terrifying, but at the same time, weirdly calm. There was not a soul around, still pitch black, besides the lights of the marina dancing on the water, as I put my paddle blade in the water. That first stroke was beautiful, soft, the blade just sliced through the morning glass like butter. It felt perfect.

The first stroke is always the hardest. Once that was done, then it was just the next, then into the next, and then… after stroke five that was it, I was gone.

I left from the marina that morning, completely alone at 4:35 am, in pitch black, out into the black open ocean, with no one around! No farewell off the dock, no flotilla of boats, no friends or family and no support team at all. Completely alone, to do something no one had done before.

Having sent the rest of the team home because of lack of funds was only one of the reasons there was no one there to see me off. The other was our concern about the security threats to myself, the craft, and the project. I wasn't able to let people know where I was in Morocco, what marina I was leaving from, and what date and time. It was all completely stealthy and under the radar. My team had instructions to wait a couple of hours after I had left before they posted anything on social media. Even more reason why I just wanted to get going. I wanted to get out into the ocean and away from all the craziness of the challenges on land. On the ocean, I felt safe and free!

I broke the marina entrance with 'Eye of the Tiger' by Survivor pushing me on. As I slipped into the deep, dark and ominous Atlantic blue and left the marina lights behind me, I passed between multiple fishing trawlers and ships on anchor waiting for first light before heading in. Before the sun poked its head over the horizon I was already miles offshore. It felt like the sunrise was greeting me with a smile, welcoming and congratulating me on the start of this epic adventure.

I let out a massive sigh and a huge 'Whoop! Yeeewww!' I had done it! I had actually made it to the start line.

Even though there had been so many obstacles and challenges to making this project a reality, so many naysayers and people with negative comments, now it was time to prove them all wrong! Over this journey I would make them all believers – believers in dreaming big and having the courage to go out there and make it happen.

# Early Days

Atlantic Ocean | 30°17'39.23"N 9°45'28.39"W

It was 10 am before I took my first 20-minute break, just under six hours into my journey. I could see the first little puffs of the onshore wind starting to ruffle the glassy sea. Conditions were about to change and I needed to shift into that next mental space.

I had accomplished the first goal: get out early and get a couple miles out before the onshore set in. Now things were about to get serious and required a different mindset to manage the next 24–36 hrs... now came the biggest test, possibly of the entire journey!

Have I got what it takes to push through what's to come? I was just about to find out if I was really as strong, as tough and resilient as I knew I needed to be and believed myself to be. This was possibly going to be the gnarliest test of my entire life, right here, right now!

I changed out my hydration packs, grabbing the last two cold ones I had prepped the day before and mixing the next two batches, as I knew it was going to be tough. I ate one of the meaty cheese baguettes I'd laid out for the first two days so I wouldn't have to waste time cooking lunches and dinners and could just go, go go... Having that foresight really helped get me through that first day for sure. Grab, eat, drink and go... until noon, when the onshore started building.

I'd been paddling for close to eight hours when I needed a proper break. I could feel it all over, I needed to calm my mind when looking at the onshore wind building. *Relax, breathe, it's exactly as forecasted would happen, we've been through this mentally already... we are good, you got this!*

I deployed the sea anchor while I took an hour break to check comms, chart my position, and do a final update on the weather before I lost cellular signal with land for good and switched over completely to satellite communications. (There is no cell signal more than five miles out here.) At least I wouldn't be drifting backwards towards land at more than 1 kn per hour, which is 1NM an hour... and it would be less than half that with the para-anchor deployed. It's all about little wins and small savings, which all add up really quickly on an adventure like this.

So, sweat the small stuff, all of it, think about and account for everything; as every little bit matters and the little things, when they add up, can and will save your life.

As I reset the parachute anchor and brought it back on board, the onshore wind came up significantly. I started paddling just after two o'clock again. I knew it was going to be pretty tough – after eight hours of paddling I was already pretty broken – so I changed down my paddle to the one with a slightly shorter shaft, with more flex and a far smaller blade. I knew paddling another 7–10 hours into a headwind for the rest of the day/night would put huge amounts of load on my body, so I needed to reduce the strain by reducing to the lowest load-bearing paddle I had and be careful not to push it too much.

This is the reason I trained with all the different paddles: I knew what to use, when and how it would affect my mental and physiological state and how it would minimize the load on my body, help me manage my fatigue, and make things easier for me in this exact situation and environment.

I pushed on for another four hours, till I really was exhausted, around six or seven that evening. I was really battling paddling into these conditions, so I put out the parachute anchor and stopped for a break, quick update and situational analysis. I'd been paddling for over 12 hours, which is like doing more than an Iron Man, except there are no water stations or changing muscle groups by switching to other disciplines or sports. But I was almost 30 miles offshore, which was a phenomenal feat really, so I enjoyed a well-deserved break with my last bit of cold hydration mix and a quick 30-minute power nap. Well, I thought I was going to have a nap.

Two minutes later, I was woken up by my AIS alarm screaming at me: two ships were bearing down on me, within two-mile range, and they were not changing course. In the middle of the night, that prospect is pretty scary. So no real sleep; my hands were really starting to ache as I got back onto the paddling shift. I put in another three hours, avoided the multiple ships before I put out the parachute again at 11:30 pm and got an hour and a half of sleep, finally.

When I woke up, I realized that I'd gone backwards by probably two and a half miles – which is about twice as much as I should have. I was frustrated, confused and a little freaked out, to be honest, as I tried to work out why that was. I looked at my instruments and it dawned on me: the difference between my distance over ground and my actual distance travelled is out by 1 kn – meaning, I'm getting hit by a current combined with the onshore breeze. That meant that even when I was paddling I was only going forward by half a knot, which is really slow – not even doing a mile an hour is super frustrating, super slow going.

It was also a pretty terrifying realization because the current was traveling directly to shore. The only solution I could come up with was pushing on and only sleeping two hours a day for the next two days until the current subsided. It really was that simple, there was no other choice or I was going to be pushed back onto land!

At sunrise I made myself a cup of coffee. The conditions were super glassy – at least the onshore breeze had died down, so that was really good news. It struck me that I had survived until the morning, over 26 hours – which is more than the Frenchman had managed.

I made some breakfast out on the little deck of my craft – coffee and nuts – and it was a beautiful start to day two. The weather conditions were really good so I cracked on. My body was aching all over and, because my hands were covered in iodized tape and gloves, I couldn't actually see the blisters, but I could feel them forming.

Day two was pretty much a copy and repeat of the day before, even though the current had subsided slightly. I paddled for almost 20 hours. There were a lot of alarms, a lot of ships that almost ran me flat. It was terrifying when they wouldn't deviate their course even after I called them on the VHF radio. More than once I ended up using my flashing laser, shining it straight at their fly bridge, where they would be piloting from, so they would definitely see me. That special laser had a military-grade light beam that would travel 5 miles, which is pretty incredible.

By the time I got through the first 48 hours I'd put 50 miles between myself and the shore, which made me feel a lot more comfortable and confident. My wind instrument had stopped working for some unknown reason; I tried to fix it, but couldn't. A couple other things had already broken, but I wanted to get through day three before I tried to fix them; 72 hours would be fix time. But thus far I'd survived the first 48 hours without getting shipwrecked on the coast of Morocco!

Goal one, milestone one, accomplished!

# Fine-tuning

I averaged 16 hours paddling each day and night for the first four days. The fourth night looked like it would be another gem, and a pod of dolphins were becoming my regular nighttime companions. I planned to paddle another eight hours that night, to try and get within 100 miles of the Canaries by the morning.

I'd had a magic moment swimming with a lone greenback turtle for 15 minutes that day. He was really slow, docile and shy, but I couldn't follow him any further than my safety tether would allow.

I believe in living each day with the courage to try something new, but there is one thing I would never risk, and that is going out on deck without hooking on the harness with its 6 ft emergency tether. It is fastened to the side of the craft and if I'm swimming I attach my 12 ft Stay Covered big wave leash, which allows me to be four meters away from my craft at any time, but not further. Using both at the same time, the one a backup to the other, when things get wild – any time the wind is over 20 kn, because if I get separated from my craft at any time, for more than 10 seconds, when the wind is over 8 kn, which is 90% of the time, the craft will drift faster than I can swim in my gear to catch it... so my percentage rate of survival, if I get separated from my craft at any time when the wind is up, is not like 20% or 10%, it's zero! I had to be vigilant all the time, every day, every night without fail.

As I neared the end of that first week I had fine-tuned some of my systems, to improve on them. But that didn't really matter, because when I was low on battery, which started becoming a regular challenge, I couldn't run my watermaker; my battery banks had to be a minimum of 80% to be able to run it and make water for an hour. That would only give me one gallon (3,8 liters) which was not enough to live and rehydrate from daily – especially while I was exercising for 16 hours plus, a day – so I had to prioritize this, as well as keeping the GPS and the chartplotter running for navigation and staying on course and then trying to keep my AIS on, so I didn't get run over by supertankers, and all the things that literally kept me alive. Once I had enough power to look after these key items and they were charged and working, I could start looking at charging cameras, phones, radio and other communication devices that were lower down on the survival totem pole.

Communications were the biggest challenge, and also my biggest comfort. I was often not able to get enough satellite signal on my little BGAN, even when the weather was good, and sometimes it would take up to an hour holding the unit up on my little deck pointing in exactly the right direction to the exact satellite to try and keep the connection for a basic and simple message to send. An hour pointing the 4 kg dish in the same direction, while trying to stay on the exact same course, imagine that!

I always find it bizarre that so many people ask if I got bored. I very rarely had any down time on my tiny little craft, between navigation, charging everything, making water and food, and prepping hydration for the next shift, and now I was also having to fit in time to fix many of the key systems and implement backups, or try and find alternate solutions to these challenges.

Within 12 hours of the start, my wind instruments failed and wouldn't come back online, but I was too focused on getting offshore over the first 48 hours to worry about it, and figured I could manage without them. Then the autopilot went down, multiple times. I had to stop and recalibrate it three times, which is not an easy simple as it sounds, especially on the first day – one of my drive arm rams for the autopilot burnt out within the first 24 hours! Thank goodness I had multiple backups, but I was starting to realize I might not have as many as I could need.

On the second day my watermaker needed to be bled; I had to run the system to get the air bubbles out, before it would work again and make water. The problem with my steering system meant that, because my autopilot failed, I had to manually foot steer, correcting my course while I was reading off my manual compass and not the electronics. I needed to figure it out, reset it all and get some rest – because I also needed to rest, reset and recalibrate myself!

When I get super frustrated and annoyed at not being able to solve something, an hour catnap (which I call a 'crabnap', because I'm a Cancerian crab) is usually enough to reset and help me solve most things.

It also helps to get out of the sun for a few hours each day, which is essential. I would use the midday peak to take a couple hours' break, to get out of the elements, grab a quick bite and get an update on weather conditions, and then head out again, a couple of hours before sunset, when the sun would be softer on my face. It was the best time to be out there on deck; before the lights went out completely and I was in the pitch black until the following morning.

I wished the wind was a little friendlier and not blowing me East, back towards Africa whenever I was off shift. My body, mind and soul needed to recover, restore and reset between shifts too, but it was hard for me to settle my mind and relax, let alone get any meaningful sleep, when I knew I was being slowly blown back towards land every time I stopped paddling!

Even if I was feeling exhausted, I would want to get up and start paddling again, because the anxiety and paranoia got me. I was still learning to master my mind and its anxiety and fears. Like everything you want to improve on in life, it is a constant work in progress; it just takes an awareness, time, focus, practice and consistency.

By the end of the first week I was 190 miles SW of Morocco. I was getting closer to the Canaries, one stroke at a time. Slowly, slowly I was catching that first monkey, Molokai style! Nothing is impossible in life, when you break it down, focus on just what's in front of you and take it one stroke at a time. If you can do that, you will eventually get there and get through anything!

Another milestone came as I passed over the Concepción Bank, 90 km NE of Lanzarote, Canary Islands, and found out that, at 193 miles, I had broken the longest solo paddleboard world record held by Bart de Zwart. Bart is a legend and inspiration to myself and so many, so I was stoked to be able to take over the baton from him and push the sport even further.

Paddling 10–14 hrs a day takes a bit of getting used to, but it's amazing what you can teach your body to do. The first three days my body really took strain, but then adjusted. It was as if it upscaled to meet its new expectations. You never know what's possible, how far you can push yourself, or how you will grow, until you try.

I started enjoying and really embracing the most amazing sunsets from my little office/SUP/home/bed all-in-one. It made me realize how little you actually need in life to make you happy.

# Dark Stormy Nights and Creatures in the Deep!

Atlantic Ocean | 29°56'37.84"N 13°40'32.14"W

On the 18th of December I was 12 days into the crossing. I was 70 miles out from the continent and looking at going right over the top of the Canary Islands.

The Canary Islands are volcanic so the shores are very treacherous, with jagged rocks. There are very few places where you safely can go in to harbor, especially with a snapped main steering system in a severe storm. As excited as I was to get to that point, after doing a weather update with Leven, things all changed. It was a pretty severe forecast; it was going to get really serious, and quickly, over the next couple of days. We had some critical decisions to make. If we got it wrong it would have heavy consequences, which I might not be able to come out of in one piece. To say it was nerve-racking would be an understatement.

This new storm approaching looked like it was going to hit me straight on, so I decided to stow everything away that I could, inside my little cabin and on deck, and brace for impact while I tried to figure out a new steering system. If I could get through the next two days, I knew it would make for some serious character-building stuff.

Looking at the big low-pressure system developing on the charts, we made the call to hold off going over the top of the Canaries, as we had originally planned. This massive storm would push me east, and east-southeast, towards the African coastline, so if I took the route we had planned I would be in the middle of the island chain and would get blown onto the rocks; there would be nowhere to hide.

But, if the *ImpiFish* and I could hold out 50 miles north of the

Canaries on the para-anchor for a couple of days until the storm passed through, and not get pushed onto the rocks at the northeastern tip of Lanzarote, once the storm had passed I should be in a good place to shoot the channel, running the gauntlet between the Canaries and mainland Morocco. Even so, the channel between the Canaries and the mainland is pretty narrow – just 20 miles wide, which was a little daunting.

The seas were starting to build and the wind was picking up pretty quick. I was nervous that I only had about 50 miles between myself and the Canary Islands, and it looked like the wind direction was going to push me directly towards them. There was not a lot I could do but hope for the best and prepare for the worst.

That afternoon there was already heavy rain and lightning. During the night the storm just got worse, with waves in the three-and-a-half to four-meter range. I got through that first night in pretty good shape, even though I didn't get any real sleep while monitoring my course, drag, speed, direction, everything, all the time, with immense stress, fear and anxiety. By the next day it had escalated to a whole other level.

I was being pushed closer to the Canary Islands every second of every minute, day and night. On sea anchor there is nothing you can do about it; when the wind gets this strong you can't paddle into it or across it. I knew that if I stayed on parachute anchor for another 36 hours I would be forced right onto the cliffs of Lanzarote. I would be lucky to escape with my life. I was literally just praying the weather would ease up before that happened – what else could I do?

That second night the swell picked up to the five-meter range, and the wind was gusting 40–45 kn. The *ImpiFish* and I were getting thrown around dangerously, we got knocked down and semi-inverted by waves multiple times during the night and almost turned completely upside down once. I'd secured everything properly, so even if I did go upside down for a while I wasn't going to be taking in water.

Even so, it was pretty terrifying inside my cabin, as there's no air (the vents have to be closed in case you go over) and this was all happening in the middle of the night, in the middle of a storm, in the middle of an ocean, in the pitch black. I could hear the waves coming, often, hitting the craft side-on, at a right angle; when they did that it sounded like a gunshot going off – Baah! The sound was so loud and violent, it felt like my little capsule was going to disintegrate around me at any moment. I couldn't help wondering whether the storm would let up before my craft either fell apart or I wrecked off the cliffs of Roque Grande off the edge of Lanzarote Island.

Every five minutes felt like an hour. I couldn't sleep for more than minutes at a time before getting hit by another wave… and then suddenly, something changed. Everything felt wrong.

The *ImpiFish* was getting jerked around strangely, pulled through the top of these giant waves, as if I was hooked or snagged on something!

It couldn't be a reef – I was 38 miles offshore. I looked at my chartplotter to work out what was going on, and pulled out my paper charts to double check the chartplotter and GPS. I was in more than 200 m of water here, so no chance of being hooked on a reef or rocks. It made no sense. Maybe it was a buoy or fishing net?

My chartplotter was telling me I was getting towed into and through the conditions, at 1,2 knots. That's not really possible! That's when I realized I was not just stuck on something, but something was probably stuck in my parachute anchor; it was jerking me around, just trying to get free.

There were only two creatures that had the power to pull me and my craft into 35 to 40 knots of wind in five-meter seas.

I was physically and mentally drained. I hadn't slept at all. But I sent a message to Leven on my satellite phone, and luckily it went through to him in Scotland, where it was still daytime. I explained the situation and parameters, and narrowed it down to one or two different things. I needed confirmation that I wasn't going completely insane. Within three minutes I got a message back from him saying, 'Yes Chris, it is either a whale or giant squid that's probably got stuck in your para-anchor. You need to take immediate action and cut yourself loose before you and your craft get taken down to the bottom of the ocean with it!'

Definitely the most terrifying digital message I've ever received!

I got into all my gear and safety harness, clipped myself on and took my time getting out of the hatch, so as not to be swamped or let any water go in the cabin. I barely had time to get out onto my deck and tether myself on before another wave hit. It was 2 am, pitch black outside with 40 knots of wind blowing like a hurricane.

I thought, *I'll just cut the one line that's attached to the mouth of the parachute anchor to open it up so the creature can get out.* But I hadn't realized how much load it would have on it; as I cut the one line, the retrieval line attached to the head of the para-anchor engaged. It spun the craft sideways, knocked me off my board and dragged me under the cold Atlantic.

I was in total blackness. The craft rolled over me and as I tried to get to the surface, I found myself trapped between the line and the center-board. The only thing I could do was reach down with the knife and cut the line. When I did it released all the tension and load instantly. I just heard this terrifying sound … Vizzzzzz … as the line spun free and tore right through my finger.

I knew it was bad but I couldn't see anything in the pitch-black chaos of the storm. I would only know how bad it really was when I could come to the surface and pull myself back onto the craft.

Thank goodness my safeties hadn't snapped – if I had been disconnected in those seas, the chance of my survival was zero. I remember being scared to look at my hand because I actually thought my finger had been ripped off. Blood was already starting to come out from my gloves. I felt through my glove to see if my finger was still attached. I was so grateful that I hadn't actually taken my gloves or oxide tape off in two weeks – that was probably the only thing that saved my finger.

I managed to grab the backup parachute anchor and deploy it, then went back down and locked myself in my cabin. When I finally got my gloves off I could see that they had saved my finger and stopped the cut from going down to the bone.

I cleaned and dressed the wound, while trying to calm down from the shock. *Keep it together bud, keep it together, it could be worse, a whole lot worse, I said to myself.*

*Relax, breathe, calm it down, slow it down, it's all good. You got this.*

I just needed to make it through another three hours to daylight. If I could rest and sleep for just half an hour, that would help my body and mind rest, recover and reset.

By daylight, things had calmed down enough for me to go outside onto my little deck safely. As soon as I went outside I realized my main foot-steering system had snapped and been ripped right off the deck of the craft. So now I had no steering, or autopilot! *Holy shit, it really doesn't get any worse than this, does it?* I was also already on my backup parachute anchor.

Then I looked up, and there in the distance I saw everything you don't want to see in that moment.

Giant waves were breaking up against the cliffs off the corner of Lanzarote, just 6–10 miles in the distance. If the weather didn't calm down dramatically within the next two hours I was going to be in grave danger.

# Threading the Needle

Lady Luck was with me – over the next three hours the weather did start getting better. The wind eased slightly and changed direction. I reckoned if I could jimmy my manual steering system and lock it in one position, I could paddle on one side only and get around the corner.

So that's what I did. The Canaries were about five miles off now. I could see the massive waves smashing up against the cliffs of the outer reef islands, amplified as the sea bottom contours became shallower. The wind had dropped to about 15–20 knots, and I found that, with the steering locked off to one side, I could angle the *ImpiFish* and paddle across the wind just enough to get past the giant cliffs.

By the time I got around the corner of the Lanzarote rocks I was two miles off – way too close for comfort and really scary. But I was finally into the channel between the Canaries and Morocco. It's a narrow 20-mile gap, which becomes really tight if the wind is blowing you in the wrong direction. The wind was predicted to pick up again in the afternoon, but I was in the clear for now. For the next 15 minutes I could breathe easy, but I still had to come up with a plan to improvise on the steering and get focused and get going to get through that channel by dark, before the wind changed direction and got too strong.

I was getting used to the manual steering system, which connected to my foot and harness, which I fine-tuned through the day. I knew I needed to figure out a better option, but right now I just needed to focus on getting through the entire island chain before nightfall.

And so I spent the next 16 hours paddling as hard as I could, not breaking for more than 20 minutes at a time. I popped out just below the bottom of Fuerteventura like a champagne cork, at about 6 pm, an hour before sunset.

Because I didn't have a good-enough steering system in place, and because of the strong wind and sea state, I couldn't go into any confined spaces, which meant I couldn't stop in at Fuerteventura to get the steering and other key items repaired. Trying to navigate into any harbor area in such hectic conditions, with so little room for error and crazy rocks and cliffs all around the entrances, without steerage or a support vessel to tow me in, would have been suicide. So I just had to get through the gap and literally thread the needle between the islands. I knew I could figure out the rest once I was clear, so that was the goal. It really was that simple.

The journey was looking like it was going to be far longer than I had anticipated. The length of time it had taken me to get to this point was almost double what I had planned, so I knew my food ration planning was out. If I was going to be short on food, I had to make the call to stop in the Canaries or continue. I knew it was too dangerous to stop, so I decided I would just have to make a plan and figure it out along the way – or simply eat less and paddle faster!

When I finally got through to the other side of the islands and clear, I did a little crab dance and laughed hysterically. I had narrowly diced with death over the last couple days, and I was still alive and basically home free. It was a huge weight off my shoulders.

I was finally through the Canary Islands. Next chance of hitting land would be in the Caribbean, 3500 NM away. Or so I thought!

# Blown Backwards

Atlantic Ocean | 27°22'31.22"N 15°37'17.47"W

After exiting the channel and passing the Canaries, I found out that I had another world first and world record, becoming the first to SUP in the open ocean, solo, unsupported and unassisted, between mainland Africa and the Canary Islands. Stoked!

I was just celebrating that small victory – you have to celebrate every small win on these kinds of journeys – but maybe I should have known better than to celebrate too soon. I was just clear of the islands and starting to feel a little more relaxed for the first time since I had left land two-and-a-half weeks ago, when I got my next weather update. All my positive thoughts and feelings changed in an instant.

There was a small depression coming from the south, from below me, that had just developed moving north. Which meant by evening the prevailing winds, which were currently behind me, were going to strengthen and change completely into the opposite direction and push me north, right back into the Canary Islands and Gran Canaria! Are you frikken kidding me?

They never get NW winds this time of the year below the Canaries, but of course this year they would, right now!

I was about 15 miles south of the island. I needed to paddle as hard as I could all day to get as far south as possible before the wind switched. Nothing else mattered. *All you can do is do the best you can, give it everything you got and then let the rest unfold the way it does.*

It was that simple.

So I gave it my all, all day, and put another 12 miles between me and the Canaries before sunset. And then, as if someone had hit a switch when the sun hit the water – click – the wind turned and started blowing me north, back towards the islands as forecast. I did another two hours' paddling directly into the conditions, fighting against the headwind, until there was no hope. I still wasn't even going forwards, I was just basically not going backwards, and I was burning myself out. By 10pm I felt broken. I was completely done, spent, depleted, nothing left. I deployed the para-anchor, went into my little cabin, to try to rest and be ready for what was to come tomorrow.

It was going to get a lot more rough and unpleasant during the night. The front brought a tropical storm behind it, with pelting rain. I just hoped I had built in enough sea room, and had to wait it out and pray I had enough favors and credits with the sea gods to let me off the hook this time.

The following morning I could see Gran Canaria again, right behind me, which was not a good thing. During the day it started getting closer and closer. By 11am, there was a slight break in the wind, down to 15kn, so I pulled up the para-anchor and paddled into it for three straight hours. I only made 500 yards forward progress, but that saved me going backwards by two miles. It's just like in life, sometimes you have to stop going backwards, before you can start moving forward again!

My next weather update with Leven was at 3pm. I prayed for better news. I was probably 10 miles offshore and if this breeze blew strong all night again, I would be on the rocks by daybreak.

I got a signal over a very broken line with Leven. 'Good news, it looks like it's going to go lighter during the night and switch back to the normal NE in the morning Chris, thank god. I was starting to wonder how we could coordinate a rescue mission from over here!'

I breathed a huge sigh. *Safe!*

Through the night it eased up as predicted. By morning the front had passed and I was greeted by light trades and blue skies blowing me in the direction of the Caribbean.

I gave thanks to the powers that be, had my morning coffee from my little press out on my tiny square of deck. I stretched and sent a

Captain's log message to the world and then got back to work paddling... This was just the beginning. I still had an ocean to cross!

I had two good days of light breeze before a later forecast warned me of a strong band of trades hitting that day. It picked up quick and stuck with me for five days straight.

Winds of between 20–25 kn, gusting 30 kn, creates a relentless and wild sea state. I was not able to get my watermaker to work in these conditions – it sucks in air as it rolls around. In addition, this band of trades brought a great deal of cloud cover, so there was very little solar to charge my batteries. There was just no time to fix any of these challenges in these conditions, not to mention how brutal it was on my body paddling day and night.

It becomes too dangerous to paddle when you are physically, mentally and emotionally drained, especially at night; that's when you get hurt, because you get careless and make mistakes. I had to be vigilant all the time, as one small mistake – like leaving the hatch open for a couple extra seconds – could cost me my life if I got caught by a rogue wave. And there were plenty of those, and this almost happened not once, but multiple times on this journey. So, sweat the small stuff, always, all the time – your life depends upon it.

# Shipping Lanes

Channel between Africa and Canary Islands
27°57'43.72"N 12°54'35.15"W

I was over 490 miles and two weeks into my journey. I may have felt home free, having come through the channel between Africa and the Canaries, but now I was slap-bang in the middle of the shipping lanes.

The marine traffic zones I would go through between Morocco and the Canary Islands and across the Atlantic are some of the busiest and most dangerous in the world. A lot of the time I was paddling at night, often when there was no moon, or no light because it was overcast, along with heavy seas and very strong winds. I knew from my 24-hour record attempts just how crazy scary and difficult it could become out there – and that was being only 5–10 miles out from solid land. Coastal waters are very different to the open ocean environment, which is a whole other world.

Months before the crossing I already started mentally preparing myself for the night paddling, in order to minimize the stress and anxiety as much as possible. I'd invested in the best systems possible to detect ships and even better ones for them to detect me. I'd made my craft as safe as possible with top tech navigational aids like a great autopilot system so I didn't have to worry about staying on course all the time, even when I wasn't paddling (which, so far, hadn't helped much at all, because it had failed). The most valuable piece of kit was the AIS – better than radar because it gives you more information on the other vessel, distance, speed, their bearings to you and potential collision ratio, in distance and time, and it does the same for them. I'd added an Echomax, to amplify the *ImpiFish*'s signal and make me look even bigger on other ships' radar. I had a VHF inside my cabin and a backup handheld outside with me on deck at all times. I had the best waterproof binoculars, with bearings and range on them, as well as two handheld compasses to check the bearings of the ships. I had the specialized waterproof military-grade laser to shine at a ship's bridge in case they got too close and weren't responding on VHF. I'd attached the Firefly strobe to the navigational pole off the stern of my craft so it was very effective. I also had various flares for emergencies.

But even with all the right equipment, the truth was I had lost steering and was traveling directly down the middle of the shipping lanes. I had no other choice.

At one point during the night four different ships were on a direct collision course with me, and I couldn't get hold of any of them. They wouldn't respond over the VHF radio. All four were supertankers almost half a mile long, each as high as a six-storey building, weighing in at 150,000 and 300,000 tons and traveling at 25 kn. There was no way they would be able to stop!

All of them came past way too close, but two of them felt like they were going to run me straight over. I could hear their engines bearing down on me. At one point my Suunto watch told me my heart rate through the night had spiked four times, over a four-hour period, to over 200 bpm, which is just short of a full blown cardiac arrest.

At night this was terrifying on a level I cannot really explain. Those supertankers wouldn't even know they had run me over. I wouldn't even be a tremor in the Captain's coffee cup, standing up on the bridge deck as he ran me flat. I would just disappear and no one would know what happened to me – another unsolved maritime mystery.

# Tilted Christmas

Atlantic Ocean | 23°0'3.00"N 22°56'53.39"W

I spent a full seven days in all my foul-weather gear, top-to-toe, pants and jacket, multiple layers, boots, beanie and gloves, with literally no break in the weather and no extra time to stop and get changed. I was just constantly cold, wet, salty, sleep deprived and completely exhausted.

I would make water and food in my tiny cabin space the size of my shoulders and only just high enough to sit up in. I had to boil water on my little open gas flame while being hammered from all sides by waves which knocked me around from side to side, trying to hold on to the boiling water for my freeze-dried food and not burn myself. I was physically and mentally drained from the multiple day and night shifts, amounting to more than 12 hours every day, all the time fighting to stay upright and not get knocked overboard by the waves and wind. And when it was overcast at night it was even more challenging and draining trying to keep my balance and just stay standing, with no horizon, no moon or stars to level me.

Christmas morning was the toughest morning I'd had on this crazy journey thus far. It was hard to get out there – it was cold, dark, stormy and scary looking, and I was broken, depleted and fatigued from the last seven days of relentless beating by the elements. I had already come off my second early shift of the morning and I was tired, low and really hungry.

I remember bringing out one of my freeze-dried food packets, tearing the top open and looking down at the same ham-and-leek mix that I hated, which I'd had literally every day for the best part of a month.

I instantly lost my appetite, even though I was really famished. Basically my body was saying, *There's no way I'm having that same packet, again!*

I started thinking of all the reasons I was doing this and tried to keep myself positive. I thought of everyone else having Christmas morning with friends and family and celebrating as I sat there all alone, and I started to feel really down.

I was in this really drained and emotional frame of mind looking out my cabin window at the intense conditions outside, when I noticed that everything looked sort of lopsided. And that's when I realized... I had a leak. I was slowly sinking!

Now, I knew I wouldn't be able to open my main deck hatches for another three days until the wind died down. That's pretty scary, knowing you are taking in water and also knowing that there's really nothing you can do about it until the weather gets better.

My mind started racing. *Am I imagining it, can that really be true? How much water have I taken on, since when, where is it coming from? Is it going to flood the rest of my compartments?* I quickly double checked my main cabin and stern cabin and they weren't leaking – good news! I opened up my back compartment and there wasn't much water at all, which was also good. But I knew it was coming in from somewhere else.

I was just trying to get my head around it, getting super frustrated and I started to get really bummed and a little emotional. *Was this crossing a really stupid idea? Why was I even doing it?* This is a perfect example of what happens when you get tired and run down. It affects your mental and emotional state and you have to catch it, have the awareness of what's happening and why, so you can remedy it and not go into a downward spiral.

*Stop it, stay focused, you're tired,* I said. *I know exactly why I'm doing this...* And then I thought of all those little children at the hospital in South Africa and how little they had, and that they'd just be stoked to have the same freeze-dried food packet I was looking at, every day. I thought of some of the other kids I met that had no arms or legs, or a little face with a mouth that worked, and then I thought about my situation with a renewed perspective. I was alive for one – that was worth celebrating, after everything I had already gone through.

I still had food, my arms, legs and mouth all worked. I needed to shut up and suck it up and get on with it, because out here in the ocean things can always be worse. Way worse!

I told myself, *Have a little bit more of an attitude of gratitude for the things you have in your life, rather than focus on the things you don't have.*

That moment became a really valuable lesson for the rest of my trip: how to bring yourself back into a more positive state. When you're lonely and you get scared and you're exhausted, don't let your mind slip into focusing on the negative things; just focus on the positive things – even if they seem trivial. The smallest positive things are all worth celebrating and being grateful for each and every day.

Sometimes you've got to just suck it up, remind yourself why you're out there, what you're doing it for. In that instant I said, *Get up, stand up, take action, make the change, be the change, make a difference!*

So I put my Santa Claus hat on, along with all my gear and harness. I went outside, got hooked in, put 'Hells Bells' by AC/DC on loud, put my head down, put a smile on my face and started paddling, knowing that every stroke I took would feed another child through The Lunchbox Fund, and roughly every 20,000 strokes would pay for another Smile operation. That right there was enough to keep me going for another seven hours, one stroke at a time.

Christmas is about counting your blessings, being thankful for what you have, including all the important and special people you have in your life, and about giving back, even though we often forget that. Take nothing for granted, ever. Even the little things.

# Desert Storm

I was still battling to manage the solar challenges, trying to figure out the best way to make it all work so that I could run all my main systems and still have enough power to run the watermaker each day. I was currently traveling almost directly south, with only a small amount of west in my course, meaning that my angle to the sun was really bad, and it would stay that way until I got to my next waypoint, 600 NM south, when I would finally be turning more west across the Atlantic.

To get any decent charging throughout the day was super challenging. I figured out that if I paddled just on the port side, meaning standing with all my weight only on the left hand side of the craft, not changing sides or strokes, it would heel over the *ImpiFish* by 8–10%, to port, which was just enough to get a better angle for the solar panels – they charged almost 15% faster with a slightly better angle to the sun.

This obviously put a lot more load on me physically, but it allowed me to make water by 2 pm, most days. That was when the batteries would get to the level I needed to make enough water for the day – but only just!

Whatever it takes to create, innovate, improvise, learn, evolve and improve to get the job done and survive – that was the name of the game and I thought I had it all figured out, until the following morning I woke up to something I never could have imagined.

The sky was weird, dense and hazy, and there was a thin red layer of something over the entire craft! What was it? I was momentarily baffled, until I ran my finger across the side of the *ImpiFish* and felt the fine grains… it was sand! Could that really be possible, sand out here, more than 500 NM off the coastline? It shouldn't be, but it was. A massive sand storm had blown in from the Sahara desert hundreds of miles across the sea, and was now blotting out the sun completely. No chance of charging my systems today, in this eerie and almost foggy red sky.

You can't make this kind of stuff up, it was insane really. I dealt with it all day. I had enough battery to just run my basic systems, but definitely not enough to make water. Later that afternoon I felt sure it would be gone by morning, so I would be fine.

The following morning I woke up to exactly the same conditions; the same dirty red sky and no sun. *What, you have to be kidding me!* There was no manual for this one. How can you prepare for this kind of extreme weather anomaly in advance, if you've never even heard of this kind of thing happening before?

This was now starting to become a serious problem and as much as I didn't want to, by the second afternoon I made the decision to delve into my backup emergency water, which is not something I wanted to do, but at least I had that option. Always have backup, because that's exactly what it's for.

I think I prayed that night that I wasn't going to be stuck inside this sand cloud for another day – and thank goodness, by the following morning it wasn't completely gone, but it had dissipated dramatically. I knew I was through the worst of it and I was hopefully in the clear enough to at least make my daily water ration!

I found out a couple of months later that this same sand cloud had travelled all the way across the entire Atlantic Ocean: the effects of it were experienced across the east coast of the USA, where it made headline news.

# Message in a Bottle

Atlantic Ocean | 16°50'23.37"N 55°36'35.88"W

One weather report can change everything, for the better or, terrifyingly, for the worse. The forecast looked a great deal better for me moving forward, which helped me stay positive through a pretty challenging period.

I'd had 15 knockdowns in the *ImpiFish*, broached twice, was thrown overboard and dragged behind the craft by my safety gear before I could pull myself back onboard. I'd been inverted once and semi-inverted twice. Half of these times had been at night.

The last time I was semi-inverted was at sunrise. I got hit by a rogue wave, side-on, while I was outside on the sat phone with Leven-the-Incredible. I got knocked overboard with the satellite phone in hand, and was dragged underwater in all my full foul-weather gear, still attached by my harness, tethered to my safety lines on deck, while trying to keep the sat phone above water to ensure I didn't lose my most valuable communication tool!

I'd now paddled over 750 km, SW since the start, and been on the ocean for just over three weeks. I was finally feeling a rhythm and routine.

This new, lighter, more steady breeze would help get me further south to the magic waypoint: 20°N 30°W, with the Cape Verde Islands 500 NM south of me into the stable trade wind zone, which should help me across the Atlantic.

I'd found creative solutions to fix many of the systems, and innovative improvements to manage others, the best I could. *Whatever makes it work and gets me to the other side* – that was the mindset and my attitude. It may not be pretty, it may not make me fast, but I'd find a way. *Whatever it takes.*

I was starting to feel better, knowing I'd got through the worst of the stormy seas and colder conditions. I was now more than five degrees south from my start in Morocco, so the water and air temperatures had become noticeably warmer. That was a huge relief. I'd been in boots, gloves and full foul-weather gear most of the time, just to stay warm and semi-dry – remember, I was only three inches above the ocean waterline, which is constantly moving and awash with waves, all the time, day and night. That meant my feet were constantly underwater, my clothes were mostly damp and I was salty and wet most of the time. Not a pleasant consistent experience, believe me.

After three weeks I took the tape off my hands for the first time. Even with the tape, and gloves over that, I had blistered massively from paddling 8–16 hours most days. I had developed calluses on my hands and fingers from them toughening up. I was still nursing the lacerations to my finger daily; because they were wet all the time, it was a battle to get them to heal, and to keep them from getting infected, but I had managed to be so vigilant with dressing my finger that it had started to heal properly too. Hopefully, in another 10 days I wouldn't be in gloves at all. Toughening up quick was key.

Even so, I had a special 'little' treat lined up for New Year's Eve.

Being out in the deep blue made me mindful of all things ocean and all things conservation, and made me think what I can do, and what we can all do collectively, to make a positive change. Most single-use plastics, like straws or plastic bags, take over 250 years to disintegrate and are swallowed up by many sea creatures, like my favorite turtle friends. So when Ardbeg whisky asked me if I could take a bottle across the Atlantic for them, I told them we had three challenges we'd need to address:

First, space is an issue as my craft is so tiny, so they would need to be mini bottles.

Second, if I only have one bottle to take across it probably won't make it to the other side, as I will probably drink it to celebrate surviving till New Year.

And third, I'm very active in ocean conservation and don't want to be seen as littering our oceans.

So, if we could put a message in a small glass bottle and send it on its way after I drink it, and make a donation to ocean conservation through the Two Oceans Aquarium, and the bottles are big enough not to be eaten by turtles, and we promote the use and reuse of glass bottles and make people aware of the damage of single-use plastics, then sure, I'd take over a bottle of the world's best single malt!

So Ardbeg gave me three tot-sized bottles, branded for the crossing. One was for me to auction off for charity on my return. The second was to go back to Ardbeg International to keep a bottle that got paddled across the Atlantic in the first ever SUP Crossing.

The last was for me to enjoy and welcome in the New Year on the 31st December. Once I had drunk it I would put inside a little message, close the cork and send it on its way.

By chance the night of the 31st December was the first night that the wind actually died. I paddled until about 4 pm, when the wind started to get super light and then it dropped to literally nothing. By six o'clock that evening, just before sunset, the ocean became sheet glass. It was beautiful, breathtaking, surreal, the best New Year's present I could have dreamed of. It was the first time I was actually able to stop and take a break and relax. So I pulled out the little mini bottle of Ardbeg.

Sometimes when you've been on a long journey towards a major goal or milestone in life, it's good to stop and reflect and remind yourself how far you have come, even if you still have a long way to go. I thought about what I had accomplished thus far. How many little kids had I hopefully helped with operations paid for, and how many fed so far on this journey… I held my little bottle up and said a toast to all of those children, and to Neptune to say thank you for keeping me safe, and for what was still to come.

I have to say that whisky was about the finest I have ever enjoyed

– and that little dram went straight to my head. I was so lean and so fit and hadn't had any alcohol in a month and I wasn't eating enough, so within 15 minutes I was pretty hammered – I was definitely the cheapest date on the ocean!

I stayed up and watched the sunset until it got dark. I reflected on life and everything that had happened so far, and everything that I was grateful for, and went to sleep. I slept like a baby from nine that night, right through until four o'clock in the morning! It was my best sleep on the entire journey. That was something to celebrate, on its own.

As for the message in the bottle, this is what it said:

*You cannot cross an ocean by staring at it, you have to get up, stand up, take action, each and every day, one stroke at a time, one day at a time, for as long as it takes in order to achieve your goals and dreams! Live each day with the courage to try... Just start!*

# Waterlogged

I had three days of decent weather and lighter winds, so I devoted any time when I wasn't paddling to searching for and fixing the leaks. I knew I was taking in water somewhere in my little craft, but I just couldn't find out where. I always look for a positive in challenging situations and the only positive I could find was that my two main compartments, where I have all my main electronics and batteries, were both dry. That was key.

This is pretty scary in itself, but more so because I was getting ready for the next low-pressure system. A small storm was scheduled to hit me on Friday afternoon, the 6th January, so I had to make the *ImpiFish* storm-ready.

This required me to move all the weight I could around, to make her more nimble and balanced. She was a little lighter, since I'd eaten a full month's worth of food, and so she was sitting higher in the water, which was positive.

I was starting to feel more comfortable and confident with my little craft, after enduring everything we had been through in our month together.

I knew the wind was going to swing SW and when the next front hit me I'd be stuck on the sea anchor going backwards for almost three days, so I paddled 12 hours, in three four-hour shifts, until just after another beautiful sunset, by which time I was completely finished, sunburnt, exhausted and broken.

The swell was starting to build, the storm clouds rolling in. The horizon loomed dark and ominous as the wind and rain started. Time to batten down the hatches. Here we go again.

I vowed to become more productive with the 'down' time; to focus on writing; fix my South African flag, which was already in tatters; give some attention to a couple of key wounds I'd acquired banging myself on everything; focus on my nutrition; repair, rest, recover and heal for a couple of days. I just wasn't getting any time to do this, so I was getting more and more depleted and my body was starting to break down. I needed to focus on maintenance of self and not only my little craft, otherwise I was going to fall apart too.

While sitting out the storm I found out that we had just reached a million rand milestone on the funding side for project. That would help feed thousands of kids through The Lunchbox Fund and pay for a hundred Operation Smile procedures over the next year. I felt so proud of how many children this project was helping.

We can all make a difference, no matter how big or how small, but we have to first take action, to make it happen. Run your own race, find and follow your passion – this will guide you to your purpose. We all have the ability to achieve all our goals and dreams, we just need to have the belief in ourselves and the courage to go after them!

As Michelangelo said, 'The greatest danger for most of us lies not in setting our aim too high and falling short; but in setting our aim too low, and achieving our mark.' Never be limited by your own habits and limiting beliefs, as we can be and do so much more.

I was on the para-anchor for 2–3 days, with the wind and storm blowing me north, instead of the direction I needed to travel, which was south and southwest. Even so, I'd paddled just over 880 miles/1360 km in 33 days, averaging around 28 miles/52 km each 24-hour period.

That left me with just over 530 NM to my next key milestone waypoint. This would get me down to 20° N and 30° W, exactly 250 miles northwest of the Cape Verde Islands, placing me right in the trade winds belt – awesome, bring it on!

The good news was that from 9 January onwards, the forecast started looking really good, with the high pressure building again and becoming more stable, which meant more consistent, constant and stable

ENE trade winds for 4–5 days, in the right direction. I hoped to cover this 520-mile distance in 12–15 days, with a daily general 24-hour projection of over 40 miles per day.

Once I reached the favorable trades, with better weather, wind and currents, my 24-hour averages should be at least 10% higher. At least that was the strategy – I still had to make it happen in reality…

After the last month of craziness, I felt like I could get through pretty much anything, but we still had a long way to go. To keep from getting overwhelmed by the massive distance and task still ahead, I took it one day at a time, one stroke at a time, just focusing on what's in front of me. Day by day, night by night, one minute at a time, one hour at a time. It's so important to break it down, to keep it simple and manageable for the mind, so you can grasp it in little bite-size chunks. *Yes, you can do this, just take it one stroke at a time, stroke by stroke and if you continue like that for as long as it takes and you never give up or give in, you will eventually get there. You'll be able to get through anything!*

Whatever time was left, I spent figuring out solutions to problems. Finally, after three days of fairly calm conditions, I found the source of the leak – or rather, *three* leak points. It was definitely a manufacturing issue, but I managed to close them with a special silicone calk sealant and a very effective two-part, quick dry, emergency epoxy I had with me for exactly these kinds of challenges. Now that I knew where they were, I could monitor and manage them. So I built that into my daily check routine. It was a huge relief not to be constantly worrying about whether I may actually be sinking.

# Taking Stock

I really enjoy the problem-solving side of things. It gives me a chance to get creative, and think out the box, because I have to. It's rewarding and motivating when you can figure out new solutions by trying to see things from multiple different perspectives. The more you test and push yourself, the more you lift your game and the better you get at it. I could feel myself learning and growing through this process all the time and I loved that. I believe we should be applying this to all areas of our lives daily, so we are constantly out of our comfort zone. Imagine if we did this all the time, what we'd be capable of?

I wanted to make the most of my down time, but to be honest there is rarely any down time when you are paddling 10–12 hours each day. On an average day I would do four three-hour shifts, three four-hour shifts or five two-hour shifts. It wasn't easy, but my body was getting used to it.

You may be thinking: but then you still have 12–14 hours remaining in 24 hours! But you'd be forgetting that I still had to manage normal maintenance checks on all systems, make water (which takes two hours), charge all systems, batteries, electronics, make food, prepare the following day's hydration, update weather forecasting and adjust routing, plot courses, while still trying to find time to do updates and capture footage, and backup everything for the film I wanted to make of this adventure. I was also doing my best to keep up with my followers on social media to let them know how and where I was. That meant writing blogs, touching base with my team, downloading footage, clearing SD cards, charging the cameras and my phone. It was just never ending really – the best words to describe it would be exhausting and relentless.

Oh, and I also needed to sleep, to recover after exercising for the equivalent of two full marathons, or an Ironman Triathlon, every day!

At the end of the next day the watermaker stopped working again too, but I fixed it by bleeding the system a couple times. Just when things were looking better, my autopilot failed again; I'd had to recalibrate it twice already to get it working and I had burnt through another autopilot ram – meaning I only had two of my original three backups left and I still had a long way to go. I'd thought I would be on autopilot 90% of the time, but now I was paddling and trying to steer at the same time which was much more effort and taxing on me as it required a lot more focus, but I couldn't risk burning through all the main autopilot backups.

When my main steering system snapped just before the Canaries, and then the other part of it got ripped entirely off the deck of my craft during the following storm, I had to jury-rig two of my own systems before I figured out one that actually worked pretty good.

The first system was just a loop I created for my foot to go through so I could pull it either way to adjust the steering left or right; I knew it wasn't ideal and just a work in progress, which was confirmed when I got caught by a wave and my foot got stuck in the loop, almost breaking my ankle as I nearly went overboard. The second system was better, more reliable and less hazardous to my health and safety, and I also added a backup; it was attached to my safety harness, so if and when I fell overboard it would pull on the steering cable, which would turn the *ImpiFish* automatically into the wind, slowing it down so that I could get back onboard more easily. It was pretty ingenious really and worked like a charm!

I'd also replaced the sea drogue anchor with my own version, which I made from various lines and then created a bridle system which seemed far more effective and efficient than the one I had purchased, and had two different levels of use, depending on the wind strength.

I created what I called my 'squiddies' – because they looked like tentacles – from different lengths and thicknesses of ropes and lines, dragged behind to steady the *ImpiFish* and help her stay a little more on course, stop her surfing when the conditions got wild, and to soften the ride of the stern of the craft – she was too light in the stern, which was also a problem for the autopilot as it couldn't keep up with her movement all the time.

My satellite phone had been overboard with me numerous times and still functioned perfectly, which was pretty incredible. The power management issue on the craft was still super challenging though. The solar panels didn't generate enough power to keep everything running and topped up – which included being able to run my basic water-maker daily (a necessity to stay alive) and my AIS and chartplotter, which kept me from being run down by multiple large tankers and ships at night. So, I had to work out which bare essentials to run when, based on potential cloud-cover reports built into my daily and weekly weather forecast, in order to deal with and manage the power issue to the best of my ability.

I would turn off some of my key systems during the day, when I was mostly on watch and paddling, to conserve them for when I was off watch and or trying to get some rest. Around 70% of the time I was not using the autopilot, so I was constantly altering my route and steer-ing manually. This meant I was zig-zagging across my course, which slowed me down and made my route a great deal longer – but it also taught me to just manage things as best I could. If you are not able to eliminate the problem completely, don't keep trying to control it. Control the controllables, do what you can with what you got and then let go of the rest, as it doesn't serve or help you mentally, so just let it go. Manage, minimize and mitigate what you can control, then let the rest go if it doesn't serve you or add value!

It still seemed like I was taking in water through my deck hatches now, so I put silicone on all the deck hatches to reduce the leaking issue, and Vaseline on all the hatch covers and their internal threads on the deck.

I finally managed to move all my extra gear, like the anchor and anchor chain and as much of the food as I could, forward to the only little extra space I had, which was under my mattress. That meant I slept on top of everything, which was really uncomfortable – but that was actually good; the more uncomfortable the better, because I wanted to spend less time in the cabin and more time paddling. I wasn't going to get across an ocean by relaxing in the cabin! So I became the squirrel that slept on his nuts (food) literally!

With the weight distributed more evenly across the *ImpiFish*, she sat a little more stern heavy in the water, which made it more manageable for the steering and autopilot (for the brief times I got it to work) but she was also now more balanced, and paddled smoother and faster.

Because my 'cabin' was so tiny, simple everyday things like making dinner or water or relieving myself were not so simple – and often took 10 times longer than at home on land. There were no taps to turn on for water, no kitchen and no toilet; the craft was tossing and rolling from side to side ALL the time with waves coming over the deck and my toilet was the sea, which at least was flushing all the time! Think about that for a few seconds – that's not just in the daytime, it was 24/7 all the time, whether it was calm or stormy, windy, rainy, day, night or frankly just terrifying conditions.

Most of this stuff we take for granted on land; it's normal and just happens. Even things like getting online to send a social media post, which I would have already written out beforehand, could take up to two hours to connect and send. Awesome as my BGAN Inmarsat system was, it needed the craft to hold its direction to maintain the satellite signal – and my little *ImpiFish* was all over the place all the time! It was still pretty incredible that I was able to post any messages to the world from out there at all, looking back at it now.

Being able to talk to people while I was all alone out there was awesome, but that only happened when the weather was really good, which wasn't a lot. In fact it was really rare. It was also a boost to receive so many messages of support when I did manage to send out messages on the social media channels. People told me they read my 'Captain's Log' ocean posts to their kids at night, to their parents – even to loved ones in hospital! Those logs regularly reached hundreds of thousands of people and the positive feedback I received from them really helped me in many ways, but also helped me feel less alone. It felt good to know I was helping people, and making such an impact and a difference.

My posts were also a way of recording mental notes and details for this book. Most of all I discovered that journaling provided welcome mental distraction from what was happening around me. A way to leave the world that I was in and connect with everyone else, myself and my purpose.

Obstacles and challenges are just opportunities to learn, change and grow. So don't fear them; welcome them as a chance to test your ingenuity and creativity, to think differently, take a different perspective, make a plan, try something new and learn from it! All these challenges gave me an immense appreciation for many of the simple things in life we all take for granted daily.

# Pfffft?

There was one gift I got to experience daily that kept me going, connected at a deep and primal level to my true self and my animal instincts, and that was the very raw, pure energy of the ocean and nature.

You have to be in it to appreciate the beauty of the deep, mystical, mid-Atlantic blue, with visibility that seems to go on down through the depths forever. It's one of most majestic blues I've ever seen – I really struggle to describe it. I wish I could beam people into this blue void, to get filled by the energy of this magical space. I find it as mesmerizing as gazing into a fire at night. Rays of light go down like fingers, so deep they feel like they have no end. It makes you feel deeply humbled and insignificant and small. Its depth and its immensity is simply unfathomable.

Over that first month, I saw pretty much most of the sea creatures people ask me about, and many more. But it wasn't like that at the beginning of the journey at all. Leaving Morocco, the water was dirty and polluted – there was plastic and general rubbish all over the place. The further I paddled away from mankind and the effects of the modern world, the cleaner and deeper the blue of the water became. The plastic issue was still deeply worrying though: almost 800 km from land I could still see plastic drifting daily. It is frightening what we are doing to our ocean and our world. It makes me very sad and equally mad!

The first two days out of Morocco, I saw no fish, except for one small-ish shark that swished by, inquisitive to see who and what I was; he followed me for a little while and then carried on his daily mission, just like me. I have the utmost respect for sharks, I'm not fearful of them, but honor them, their beauty and their majesty in the ocean. These amazing creatures are so horribly misunderstood. They've got a bad rap from society and films like *Jaws,* that have programmed humans into being fearful of a beautiful and highly necessary animal which keeps the balance of all creatures in the ocean food chain and ecosystem.

As an ambassador for Cape Town's Two Oceans Aquarium, I had the chance to free-dive with the aquarium's ragged-tooth sharks. It was one of the most awesome experiences of my life. It proved to me yet again that, when it comes to the animal kingdom, if you act in the right way and send out the right energy and signals, if you are aware and remain calm within your body and mind and let them know you see them, and understand that you are in their space and environment, you will be fine. If you don't act like prey, then you won't get treated like prey. Since this experience I've free-dived with many sharks and have learned to become more comfortable in their space, respect them and understand their behavior better.

On the second evening out from Agadir I saw a small pod of about eight dolphins, which always make me smile and give me so much joy. I saw them every evening while I was frantically paddling to try to get away from land, and because I was stressing for my life, I wasn't really appreciating the dolphins as much as I normally would have.

Dolphins are sentient beings. They are among the most intelligent mammals on the planet, and they can hear, feel and read your emotions and energy. It was only weeks later that it dawned on me: the dolphins were picking up my stress and anxiety, being alone and afraid. I believe they were just coming by to check in on me to make sure I wasn't alone. They came back every day for the first seven days straight. Once I had created a 60 NM buffer, and wasn't stressed anymore about being blown back onto land, I never saw that pod again. I believe they felt my tension easing and knew they weren't needed any longer. That's pretty deep, but deep down I know it and believe it.

The connections and experiences I started having out there in my new and wonderful blue world were next level. I believe we are connected with all creatures in our environment. Connected to a deeper universal energy, which I call the source. We just need to be able to read, feel and understand all the signs around us.

And I was getting better at this every day. It was like unlocking the code, like reading the matrix; once you see it and feel it, a whole new world opens up to you. And a big part of this is the ego, being able to let go of this, not trying to control everything and just surrendering to the present, in order to be in flow. Focused only on the now, only on what's in front of you, connecting to your surroundings and just letting go!

Over the following week I saw all different kinds of dolphins, which was a joy and a gift, as they really are some of my favorite creatures on the planet. I saw spinner dolphins, duskies and bottlenose dolphins, and also, sporadically, small fish, and a green sea turtle who came by briefly for a visit. The turtles became almost a daily sighting as the water started getting warmer, the further south I travelled. I also got to swim with a loggerhead turtle, which made my day. I was super stoked, even if he wasn't that keen to hang around for very long. He was just chilling, not swimming much, just hanging out and enjoying life, being a turtle in the big blue sea. I think I was too excited and scared him a little jumping in too quickly. My excitement for turtles does sometimes get the better of me! They are called 'tartaruga' in Portuguese – my favorite word!

I had had amazing encounters paddling under the moonlight, as I watched it dancing on the deep, dark ocean canvas. I found myself constantly whipping out my GoPro to get footage of my little dolphin friends. Most of the time it was too dark for the camera to capture them playing under the stars next to me, but they brought me great joy and comfort, these regular visitors to my moonlit night shifts.

On New Year's Day, there wasn't a breath of wind. It was flat calm – the first day like this in five weeks, and there was no moon at all. I was paddling slow and steady through the eerie silence, it was so beautiful and strange at the same time. There was nothing besides the sound of my blade and the soft trickle of my craft moving through the ocean blue – until suddenly, there was something else.

At first I thought it was my jacket rubbing against the side of my ear, or brushing my side as I paddled, but then I stopped paddling to check and sure enough, there it still was.

It continued, every two to three minutes… *Pffft*… The sound came out of the low dark haze over the water, reflecting the beautiful twinkly night sky. And it was moving closer.

I became a little nervous and spread my stance to get more stable, just in case. Whatever it was had come within 10 meters of me. *Pffft*… By now I knew most of the oceans sounds, but this was a new one, something completely different.

All of a sudden I was surrounded by about a dozen small whales. I never got to actually see one properly, as it was a pitch black night with no moon, but I could hear them surfacing and breathing all around me for almost half an hour. It was incredible, like they were just keeping me company. It felt like I had my own personal silent, stealthy, nighttime whale escort. It was literally breathtaking, and surreal, at the same time. Their sounds resonated right through me and filled the night sky and dark waters of the deep, crystal clear and as loud as the depths of night.

I will never know what went '*Pffft*' in the night, but that's okay. It just made me realize how incredibly special those unique moments are, and how few people on this planet ever get to experience something like this. Being able to let go and just be immersed in it, completely unafraid, savoring every sound, like an orchestra of sensory overload, as these creatures swam, dived and glided around me was an experience I will never forget.

Any chance I get to swim with ocean creatures I'm over the side and in the water, especially if it's during the day and calm seas, as that's so rare and unique. Connecting with nature is simply the most pure, raw happiness you will ever experience as a human. When you're swimming with dolphins or whales you can really feel that connection deeply, if you free your mind and yourself, allow yourself to let go, be one with it, connecting on a far deeper level and be let in.

# My Favorite Blues

Atlantic Ocean | 19°16'14.31"N 40°39'1.65"W

The next afternoon I got to see my favorite creatures on my journey, which I had been spotting briefly in flashes over the last week or so. But that day a school of yellowfin tuna swam with me for a good 15 minutes. I had come to know them as my 'Flashes of Blue & Yellow' or my favorite Blues. They have these incredible colors, they almost seem to glow, with these electric blues and bright neon yellow.

Over the next three weeks the flashes of blue and yellow came back in a smaller school, but came to swim with me almost at the same time each day. What made it even more special and unique was that they seemed to somehow adopt me as the leader of the pack and line up in formation with me on the *ImpiFish*, like in a squadron of fighter jets, four or five of them on either side of me. After a while of swimming next to me in formation each day, the one alpha of the school would make eye contact with me, as if to ask permission to go off and hunt and they would suddenly break away, out of formation and all speed off into the deep blue. Within seconds you could see flying fish jumping out of the water all over the place, as they were hunted down ahead of me. It was such an incredible connection, such a sight to behold. I will always feel so grateful to have had these truly remarkable and unique experiences, which very few humans ever get to witness. I will cherish those deeply transcendent and magic moments for the rest of my life.

The next day, the wind was still super light. I was trying to make the most of these conditions to fix any major issues before things got wet and wild again – which was the only constant I could be sure of. I was shuffling things around to redistribute the weight around my craft again as things had progressed in the two weeks since the last weight rebalancing, when I started having that horrible feeling again, that I was listing to one side. I thought, *This can't be, I fixed all the leaks, and I've been monitoring everything so that can't be possible...* But sure enough, on closer scrutiny, I was listing to the port side.

The first ever SUP session off Nelscott Reef, Oregon.

The first ever SUP session off Dungeons, South Africa.

The winning wave of the Mavericks Big Wave Invitational, 2010, California, USA.

At the finish of the 12-hr Open Ocean World Record paddle, crossing the mouth of Langebaan Lagoon entrance with passing oil tanker!

The start of the 12-hr World Record paddle, with whales in the background – a perfect day.

STANDUP PADDLING (SUP) 11:59'59.6
Open Ocean 12 Hour SUP World Record 17 Dec 13

new    record    world

| Heart rate (88-174) | Distance | Speed (max 25.2) | Recovery time |
| --- | --- | --- | --- |
| ♥ 130 bpm | ▭ 130.11 km | ⊙ 10.8 km/h | ⊚ 120 h |

| PTE | Calories | Temperature (17.2-23.8) | Est. VO2 |
| --- | --- | --- | --- |
| PTE 3.8 | 🔥 4289 kcal | 🌡 20.4 °C | VO₂ 44 ml/kg/min |

| Easy | Moderate | Hard | Very hard |
| --- | --- | --- | --- |
| ♥ 0:41'21 | ♥ 6:23'35 | ♥ 3:50'52 | ♥ 1:02'08 |

| Maximal | EPOC Peak | | |
| --- | --- | --- | --- |
| ♥ 0:02'04 | EPOC 152 ml/kg | | |

⌃ Less

The 12-hr World Record paddle statistics.

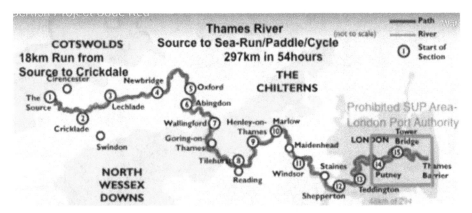

The route and plan for the first ever Source-to-Sea River Thames expedition: 297-km Run/ SUP/Cycle.

The start of the Source-to-Sea Run section, which started in the Cotswolds, under an old ash tree.

The need for wind and speed, deep in the Namibian desert, at the Lüderitz Speed Challenge.

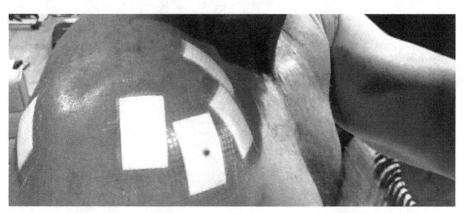

The final shoulder surgery before the SUP crossing, which was nerve racking.

A happy face as my little craft the *ImpiFish* finally arrives in Morocco.

Team work makes the dream work: Leven Brown and I on the Agadir dock days before leaving.

Solo and alone, early morning at the start of the SUP crossing, from Agadir Marina, Dec 6th 2016.

Stripe the fish, my greatest companion for the entire journey.

A bad Christmas, made positive with an attitude of gratitude.

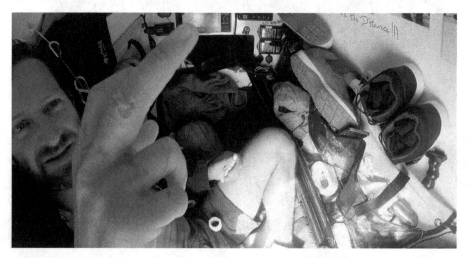

My badly cut finger, from when I was trapped under craft in the storm.

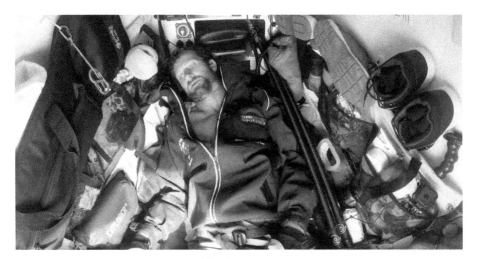

Exhausted inside my tiny cabin, after a heavy and intense night!

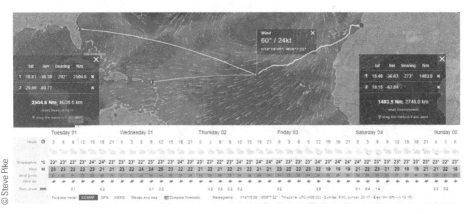

The midpoint, choices and course change.

Mr Wings the flying fish, who made me so happy.

ABOVE In flow on my morning underwater glide.

LEFT My favorite 'Blues' – the beautiful tuna fish.

BELOW A bad day at the office, cutting away lines from the consequences of the centerboard storm problems.

One of the many turtle friends I met on the Atlantic crossing.

The same freeze-dried meals, every day for 3 months – very unpleasant.

The lonely yet perfect bluebottle, all alone in the Atlantic blue.

Any time you're pumping water out from your craft, that's a serious problem!

This little pufferfish was a positive and friendly visitor in a challenging time.

Weather updates on the satellite phone with Leven Brown.

24-hr Open Ocean Record broken, so celebrations must be had.

Air guitar and the dancing sea pirate.

Becoming the Squall Rider!

Paddling north across all the challenging conditions damaged my shoulder even more.

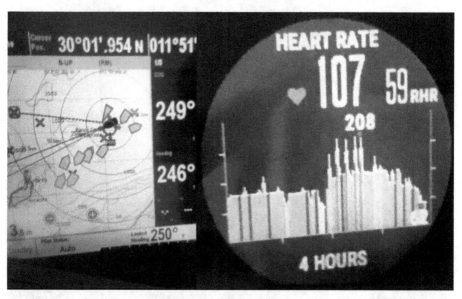

My Garmin watch heart rate and the screen showing all the ships passing me through the shipping lanes!

Bury the bow and keep riding and surfing.

A mighty claim and celebrations after almost being rolled by a big wave, while coming in to Antigua.

Managing to surf the *ImpiFish*, completely at ease, in flow, while in crazy conditions.

Triggering the final finishing flare to celebrate the end of the journey, triumphant, beneath the 'Pillars of Hercules' cliffs of Antigua.

This image sums up the final day and the conditions I had been experiencing alone for 93 days.

Finally stepping onto land – let the celebrations begin! Mission impossible, just made possible.

A shoot done after the crossing was complete showed how my body and face had changed from 93 days at sea.

# 101 Ways with Vaseline

Before the wind started picking up as the next front was about to move in, I got out the special hatch spanner to open the deck hatch I had to put my whole weight into it . – *Holy shitballs!* Water, a LOT of water.

That's a huge problem and that is where the issue was right there – those are meant to be watertight compartments, and my food was in there too. I scrambled to get my food packs out as quickly as possible to see how many were damaged. At least three taped-together packs were waterlogged... that's three full days of food gone! I didn't have the capacity to carry extra days of food, and it had already taken me far longer to get past the Canary Islands than I'd planned, so I'd already gone through the buffer of food rations I'd built into the trip, as a backup. That meant I was now short on food for the time remaining on the sea – assuming things went well! And we know how that works out here in the ocean... 'F*******ck!' I cursed out loud, at myself, at the craft, its builders, at everything!

I pulled everything out, as quickly as I could, grabbed the emergency water pump and start pumping frantically to get the water out and find out where it was coming in from.

I had pumped out about 12 liters (3 gallons) and as I was still pumping, with the pipe from the pump swishing around in the water over the side next to the rail of the craft, when suddenly out of the corner of my eye I saw something weird, yet wonderful, that distracted me.

*What is that thing?*

It was the cutest little creamy-white, spotted, square-shaped pufferfish, one of my favorite fish on the planet, trying hard to keep up with me and catch the swirling, swishing bubbles coming out from the pipe… I laughed out loud. *'That's funny'* I said, and smiled in the middle of the chaos!

I got out the GoPro and started filming him in the water, under, over… he was just on a mission to catch the end of the bilge pipe. It was so beautiful to capture some amazing footage of one of my favorite little sea creatures swimming around in his happy blue home, all alone, just like me…

What a treat! It was such a special little moment, where I was almost lost in time and forgot about the leak in the craft.

It completely stumped me; it was a watertight compartment so where was the water coming from? Then the realization set in: the only place it could be coming in was through the hatch lid – but it couldn't be, it looked perfect and had been super tight…

But that was the only place it could be coming in as it was now empty and I could see there were no holes and it's a completely watertight compartment, so the only way it could possibly be leaking was through the gasket seals around the lid cover; they had to be leaking. The deck of my little craft is only three inches above the waterline, so, there was a lot of water washing over the deck all the time. It was just slowly leaking in through the gasket, drip by drip; after more than 40 days, that added up to 15 liters of accumulated water, which was a massive problem. Suddenly the fear and dread set in, *Oh no, could all of them be leaking like this? Solutions, solutions… Think Bertish think! Gaskets, gaskets…*

The Vaseline for my bum – which I'd been advised to bring for chafe, but hadn't yet used – was perfect for greasing the gaskets. I had one spare hatch cover that I could pull out as a backup, I'd go through each and every hatch – four deck hatch covers – to ensure the others weren't leaking either. One thing I could not afford was more damaged meal packets. After this issue, I was going to be on rations for the rest of the trip, which was a scary realization so early on. Especially as I had already lost a lot of weight and I wasn't even halfway across yet!

# Shift Happens

The following morning started out beautiful and glassy, and I was feeling a lot better after sealing the hatch gaskets. Awareness is the first key to success; action, innovation and creativity are the next. Then keep monitoring it and keep moving forward. I had amended it the best I could.

There was zero breeze for the first two hours, and as I was paddling through my second shift I saw something strange on the surface. It was small and transparent, off a little ahead of me and hard to see. The water was glassy and clear and merged with the horizon, so it was a little deceiving on the eye, but became crystal clear as I got closer and it floated past, literally two feet away from me: a crazy magnificent bluebottle, out there in the middle of nowhere.

I caught myself saying, *What the hell are you doing all the way out here, all alone buddy?* Then I thought, *I guess it's all relative, the bluebottle could probably be saying the same thing about me.* I laughed out loud. These are the little things you find amusing out here alone, in the middle of the ocean, and these are the creatures you have conversations with.

I even composed an 'Ode to the Creatures of the Deep', and posted it on my blog:

> *I believe in the sea & its creatures within, it's who I am,*
> *I am the sea and it is me. I feel you near, I breathe your*
> *energy and hear you speaking in your squeaky language,*
> *through the walls of my little craft... I feel your presence*
> *deep within, sometimes I hear you, even if often I don't*

*see you, but just the knowing comforts me, it guides me,*
*it softens my worries and lightens the load. Thank you for*
*your love, your guiding light, your positive presence, your*
*constant support, lessons, and friendship, it's helped me*
*more than you will ever know...*

I had now been out on the Atlantic, alone on the *ImpiFish*, for exactly 40 days.

I wanted to reach the transatlantic waypoint of 20° N 31° W by the next week, so I really needed to chew through those miles as fast as I could. While the weather was favorable, I increased my daily shift hours from 11 to 13 hours of paddling a day, which gave me less time for writing. Even so, I tried to write at least once a week. *Bear with me world, I'm busy paddling across an ocean...*

Two weeks into January, the fair weather gave way to the predicted storms. I spent a full-moon night paddling through crazy squalls that came in with little warning besides a scary, ominous, dark line on the water and billowing black rain clouds that moved in quick and were hard to see coming in at night. By the time you see them, they're on you within seconds.

I also had a one-knot current running against me, for almost two days, putting massive strain and load on my body, physically as well as mentally. It really made forward progress super challenging – it just wears you out and wears you down, as you work so hard and make very little progress, while depleting yourself in every way.

I am always super hard on myself with the goals and targets I set. But when conditions change without warning, like the adverse current, you have to just learn to be a little softer on yourself and give yourself a break. I believed that I would get to my target, but it was going to be in nature's time and not on my schedule. Nature doesn't fit into your time frame and you need to always remember that, as it's the one thing you can't control.

Learning to let go of control and making peace with that was the hardest thing to do. It sounds easy in principle, but when you're already low on rations it's a lot more challenging to implement in practice.

Since I left Morocco, I'd noticed some dramatic shifts in my consciousness. It was fascinating to move into a new mindset; to see how it enhanced my progress and capabilities was awesome. I was ready to shift further; life is all about continuously learning, growing and evolving, wherever and whenever possible. I even came to love seeing ships and interacting with them, so much that my night shift paddling became my favorite time of my 24-hr period! As Wayne Dyer says, 'change the way you look at things and the things you look at change.' So true!

We all have things we fear and we all don't like being pushed outside of our comfort zone because it's exactly that – uncomfortable! I'm not superhuman or any different to anyone else out there, but I've learned that *this* is where the magic happens. It's where growth, inspiration and your greatest learning comes from, and it's where your greatest self and potential lies. Once you've faced your fears and you are able to move through them, you start to welcome and actually encourage constant change in your life, and that mental shift in perspective and mindset changes everything. It makes it exciting, keeps you creative as you are constantly learning, growing and evolving, so you are constantly inspired.

Over the years I've applied a very simple philosophy to everything: the more you do something, the more you do anything in life, the better you get at it and the better you get at handling and dealing with any situation. Discipline, consistency and repetition builds habits and makes you more comfortable with a situation; eventually it becomes your norm – which means you are ready to shift again and grow further. It's also all about attitude and mindset.

I shifted my comfort zone in three stages: I mentally prepared beforehand; I forced myself to do it over and over again (repetition); and I learned to reprogram my mental state to genuinely love it, which shifted my mindset and enabled me to grow even further. It's always been the same for me. My progression into surfing bigger and bigger waves, was the same. It didn't just happen – you don't just wake up one day as a big wave rider! It was a slow, focused, consistent progression of shifting my comfort levels and growing each time.

I learned how to reduce the stress, handle the anxiety and manage the fear. And then I learned to use the fear as a tool, as my friend, and harness its power. I became better prepared, with better equipment and better physical and mental preparation and very specific, focused underwater training, which I developed myself, in order to give me the mental confidence to push it further. Over time, I developed more knowledge and experience to handle situations better, which allowed me to surf and feel more confident and comfortable in bigger and bigger waves.

I try and work with and around the conditions, to create or manipulate them to my favor and then put myself in that uncomfortable space as much as possible, until the uncomfortable, almost becomes your new norm. Then you learn to manage them and respond to those situations even better. Deal with the things you can control, control the controllables, manage the ones that you need to, minimize the things you are not able to control, then analyze the situation afterwards to see what you could have done better. Most importantly, grow from the experience. Evolve and move forward again. That way you can apply the knowledge next time around. The more you put yourself in that space, with the right attitude and mindset, the better you will get at dealing with it and the better the outcome will be for you every time.

Out in the ocean, when the nights were cold, dark and windy, the hardest thing was to silence that little voice in my head trying to talk me out of getting up and going outside for the next shift.

But you have to learn how to control and master that little voice, and not let it control you. I would stop it in its tracks and override it with a more positive power sentence like: *Get up, stand up, get out there, take action, make the change, be the change, now! Right now. Go!*

Every surfer knows the feeling when it's cold and windy and the surf is not great; you're sitting in your warm car and your little voice starts talking you out of going for a surf. The longer you sit and don't take control of it, the less likely you will be able to control it. Catch it, override it and just go – take action, now!

When have you ever gone out for that surf and then regretted it afterward? Looking back, you're always thankful you did go. There is literally never a time, you look back and say, *I wish I hadn't.* The positive endorphins kick in and make you feel energized and alive, alleviate stress and make you healthier and happier and you know afterwards, that it was a good idea and you never regret it, you're just grateful you did!

Remember that, and apply it to everything. You are the master of that voice – don't let it master you!

# Golden Monkeys

I often have people comparing what I was doing to rowing on a rowboat or a surfski, and I always feel the need to correct them. There is a massive difference, which most people don't understand unless I explain it. What I was doing was far more challenging in three very distinct areas.

Firstly, rowers are sitting down, all the time! Which means they never have to worry about the balance aspect. The first thing you lose when you get cold or fatigued is your balance. This is no problem when you're sitting down, but staying upright is the greatest challenge when the waves are constantly tipping your little board. In the daytime, it's like standing on a big yoga ball, but at night it's even more difficult; when the light goes you lose your horizon, which means you instantly lose your balance. That's even more of a problem when you are paddling in crazy winds and seas. I basically had to learn how to paddle by braille, using my other senses and developing new ways to keep my sense of balance and paddle by feel, instinct and intuition, which is even more exhausting when you are tapping into and relying on these extra senses.

The second big difference is that rowers have two oars, whereas I only had one paddle shaft and blade.

And the third is that rowers are on far bigger crafts, which are wider, longer, heavier and far more stable. By way of comparison, a rowboat is between 22–40 ft (7–12 m) long and 6,5–13 ft (2–4 m) wide, sitting 2–4 ft (0,6–1,2m) off the water; my craft is just under 5,5 m/19 ft long and 1,2 m wide and my deck is three inches above the water – which means that where I stand and paddle is wet, or under water, most of the time.

Rowers are also protected from the ocean by the freeboard, meaning they sit higher above the water and are protected from the elements by the higher side rails and the main cabin, which shelters them from most of the weather and waves; because of this they rarely get very wet. And they are mostly in teams of two, four, six, eight or even 12 persons.

When you're alone, and you're standing, your balance is tested every split second, as the craft moves under your feet all the time, and when it's pitch black and you have no visual sight and no horizon… that, my friends, is a very different and way more challenging and exhausting experience.

If you're wondering why I'm going into so much detail about rowboats, it's very simple.

I've mentioned before that Leven was a veteran ocean rower with a couple world records (including a Guinness World Record) to his name. To say the guy is a legend is an understatement.

Eight days before I reached the top of the Canary Islands, Leven told me about a transatlantic rowboat race that had just started from Gran Canaria, off the bottom of the island chain. He just mentioned it in passing, since it's always interesting to know which other vessels are out there, besides yourself. But I saw a golden opportunity.

The Talisker Whisky Atlantic Challenge starts in the Canaries every two years, and ends in the Caribbean. The race teams of mostly twos, fours and sixes were all in pretty big boats – double to triple the size of my little *ImpiFish* – and they were fast, with multiple people paddling all the time. They also have a support vessel that follows the fleet in the distance, and it's a shorter distance, and it's rowing – but it's still always an impressive feat for anyone who completes it. Huge respect always.

Because I left from Morocco 500 NM further north, the race had already started this year, but I didn't know it until Leven mentioned it. The rowers were already nine days ahead of me before I even got to their start point. But from the moment Leven told me about the race, I asked him to keep me informed about where the back of the fleet was.

Ever since my Molokai race I've lived by the phrase 'Slowly, slowly catch a monkey!' to help me focus on what's in front of me and also to help give me motivation. For the next weeks I used the back of their fleet as my 'one golden monkey', my key mental carrot, to keep pushing me harder. It became my focus to see if I could catch up to or even pass just one of the rowboats on this journey, before I got to the other side of the Atlantic. I knew it was a long shot, but I had to have something to aim for, so why not aim high and just try?

You become what you think about and focus on all day long. I know this and live by this and have re-affirmed it all my life.

# Prepared for Anything

When the conditions got challenging, I'd go into what I call PFA mode: Prepared For Anything. It's when I tell myself to shut up, gear up, get out there and make it happen.

I've talked about the shut up part – mastering the voice that tells you to stay cozy and embracing the benefits of getting out there and taking action instead.

But that doesn't mean putting yourself in unnecessary danger, or even discomfort. That's where proper planning and preparation, mindset and attitude come in – and the right gear is key.

For the night shifts, I would set the goal, the target number of miles I needed to attain on the chartplotter, and then I would get into my PFA gear – which wasn't a simple task in my tiny little cabin space. Sometimes it could take up to 15 minutes to get into all my gear, the same applies when coming back in from my shift. So that's half an hour used up right there. When I attained the number I had set for myself, no matter how long it took, only then could I go back into my little cabin that night and have a hot meal as my reward.

Starting from the bottom up, I'd put on:

1. Waterproof socks, sometimes two pairs
2. Gul Gore-tex thermal inners
3. GXC boots
4. Gul Code Zero sailor foul-weather bottoms (Salopettes)
5. Thermo shirt

6. Gul Code Zero offshore sailing jacket
7. Zinc oxide tape for hands
8. Gul gloves
9. Waterproof beanie
10. Mini head torch
11. Main deck knife
12. Skeletool knife – attached to my harness
13. Mini Firefly torch
14. Emergency strobe
15. Harness
16. Carabiner – clipped to the safety tether
17. Big wave leash connected to my ankle
18. Hydration pack (and backup pack)
19. Snacks
20. One large cup of coffee

In fact, it took me so long to get in and out of my PFA gear that when the conditions were intense I started to sleep wearing most of it, as I just couldn't waste 15 minutes getting in and another 15 getting out of gear, especially when things were tough and I was going backwards.

I had done this PFA ritual for well over a month, in all kinds of weather, most of it foul, when finally Leven gave me a decent weather forecast: a full week of great wind and weather, 10–15 kn in the right direction, NE and E. It was the first positive long-range forecast since I had left Morocco, over 42 days ago!

During that fairly calm weather stretch I had one particularly epic night. I did two shifts, from 7–9:30 pm and again from 12:30–4 am, with a perfect clear night sky, an almost full moon, and incredible phosphorescence in the water lighting my path. I was immersed in this glowing magical tapestry, a swirling artwork in the water all around me and next to me with every stroke of my paddle, it was magical. As if that wasn't enough, I saw multiple stupidly bright shooting stars throughout my shift. It was like something out of the movie *Life of*

*Pi*. It is hard to do justice to it with words. I was left spellbound and entranced by the beauty surrounding me. I felt equal measures of gratitude, wonder, bliss and awe at the incredible experience, so raw, powerful, perfect and pure. People say 'follow your bliss'; in that rare magic moment, I was living exactly that.

At the end of my shift, I lay back down on my little solar panel at the stern of my craft for a full hour just writing notes. I started updating my 6-year plan, which evolved into a crystal clear 10-year plan. I went from Thought to Idea to Dream to Vision to Mental Picture to a Literal Visual Road Map and Timeline with Goals and Action Points.

Dream it, see it, believe it, achieve it. I've made this my mantra: I live by it, and it's never let me down.

I should have been tired, but I wasn't at all. I couldn't even keep up with my fingers typing furiously – if a little clumsily in my paddling gloves – in the dark, but under the magic light from the sparkling stars.

I remember thinking, *I still need to be up at sunrise for my weather update*. It just shows that passion for what inspires you truly does transcend fatigue – it transcends anything. It actually gives you more energy – when you are truly inspired, there is no such thing as tired and nothing you cannot achieve!

I've learned to love the night. It's the time when my thoughts and ideas are the most calm and clear; it is peaceful, with little to no distractions or clutter.

And it definitely helps to be thousands of miles from the nearest land with no other human being in sight!

# Staying Alive

Atlantic Ocean | 18°37′40.00″N 46°55′5.99″W

For most of my adult life, I've weighed in at about 75 kg (165 lbs), but before this trip, I wanted to bulk up and gain an extra 5 kg. That proved more difficult than you would imagine – I was training so much I just burnt everything I put in! So a month before leaving, I stopped training completely and that really helped significantly. I reached 80 kg just before I left and went up a pants size, but by the end of the crossing I had dropped more than two sizes, from a size 32- to 28-inch waist.

Anyone keen on the Captain Crabstick Adventure Diet Program, just spend three months eating 6,000-8,000 kilocalories a day, exercise for 11–16 hours per day to burn about 10,000 kcal, and I'm pretty sure you'll drop a quarter of your body mass. It's definitely not a diet for the faint hearted!

By mid-January my Garmin Fenix watch, which monitors my stroke rate, told me I had paddled over 1,045,000 (one million forty-five-thousand) strokes. I had dropped close to 10 kg. I knew I would probably lose another 5–10 kg over the next 45 days.

Food and hydration were key to the project, but also super challenging. It started with the major hiccup we had just before leaving, when the freeze-dried food sponsor I had lined up went bankrupt two days before I was supposed to collect all the food for the journey and we had to scramble to make an emergency plan with another supplier.

I wasn't even sure what freeze-dried food I was getting until opening the boxes that arrived a week before departure. Remember, there were only three different types of meal packs for over 95 days, and two of them wouldn't have been something I would have chosen at all. But this is what happens on big projects like this; when you get hit by massive curve balls, it's just your attitude and how you react to it that matters, that's all you can control. You have to breathe deeply, try to learn from the experience and do the best you can with what you've got.

We'd sorted my freeze-dried meal options into daily ration packs, all tied together with duct tape inside a Ziploc bag. There were 95 packs for 96 days, which was our worst-case-scenario estimated time to the Caribbean. Each pack had three freeze-dried meals: ham pasta (Carbonara), ham-leek with mash, and my favorite (not!) Nasi Goreng. I found out within the first five days that the Nasi Goreng was giving me the runs. So I was down to two of the exact same meals a day for 90–95 days straight!

After 30 days my body and mind were over it and started revolting. I had to stop and catch myself getting negative when that little voice started taking control.

As the amazing Albert Einstein once said, 'You can't solve a problem with the same mind that created it!' Change your mindset and what you see will change. I needed to think out the box. How could I solve this?

Solution number one is always: get some rest. A couple hours of sleep helps me reset and re-focus so I can look at things from a fresh perspective and make better decisions. There is always more than one solution to every problem; I came up with a creative solution to mix up the meals and voila, five new dishes for me.

I used different combinations of the two meals I did have, and added mixed nuts, or sometimes biltong (beef jerky), and mixed my favorite dish with my worst one to make it more palatable. I also had two big bags of powdered mashed potato, as an extra for whenever I would need it later in the journey. After 40 days out, this mashed potato powder proved invaluable; I added it to many of the meals for variety and to make them more substantial. Problem solved right there, just by shifting the perspective and with the right attitude!

The Ziploc bags we had attached to the daily ration packs included a rehydrate sachet, to add electrolytes to the water for better hydration; an Enduren energy cocoa or date bar; two Racefood (nougat) Fast bars and Far bars, which are special quick and slow energy release bars for endurance racing (all amazing – I'd been using them for the last couple of years); some chopped up biltong; and a mini bite-size chocolate.

Every now and again I'd find my team had added a funny little note into random meal packs, just to make me smile, which was awesome. The power in a good team! Those little things really did help out there and kept me going through the worst times, while I was all alone.

Finally, I had a couple of big bags of mixed nuts and dried fruit for variety. This also worked really well; I left most of this for later in the trip as a reward and a treat, for when I reached certain key milestones.

I cooked all my food on my mini Jetboil gas cooker, which is amazing. It fits into the palm of your hand and is a camper and adventurer's best friend. I had packed 12 mini gas canisters to get me through my journey and three gas lighters; even though the Jetboil has an auto-ignition system, they never last more than a couple months, so as with everything, I always have multiple backups!

Water was a whole story in itself. The mini electric-powered Katadyn desalinator sucked water in through a port in the side of the craft and removed the saltwater through reverse osmosis under pressure, which turned it into fresh drinkable water. It would take an hour and a half to make one gallon (3,8 liters). I lost count of the hours I spent outside on my little deck watching it decant painfully slowly into a gallon container, drop by drop, ensuring every second that no outside seawater splashed into the container at all during this process.

As a comparison, most ocean rowboat teams budget for 10 liters per person, per day – six liters for drinking and four for washing and sanitary use. I didn't have that luxury as I was only able to make five liters most days, six when I struck it lucky on an epic sunny day and all systems were good.

Like most things on my tiny little craft, there was a catch – actually a couple of catches – with this essential yet tricky little unit. Firstly, I wasn't able to use it in stormy conditions; when the craft rolled around a lot, the inlet hole would suck in air and I would have to bleed the entire system, which was difficult to do. It used a lot of power to do this and while I was bleeding the system it wasn't just using up the power I had allocated to make my daily water rations that day, it was also not making any water!

Secondly, the watermaker needed a great deal of power to run, and I ideally needed a minimum of three gallons of water per day to survive when paddling 10 hours plus, which meant running it for at least four hours a day, which I could not do, as I could only run the system if things were good for a maximum of 1–2 hours a day to make 1,5 gallons and only when my battery banks were more than 75% full, which only happened – if I was lucky – at the hottest time of the day when the sun was strongest.

The power management issue was a sharp learning curve for me, with two of the key systems drawing more power than they were supposed to. I figured out a bare-bones, daily power plan for the essential systems, which I still needed to use when conditions were overcast; then, on a perfect day with no cloud cover, I could use more of the non-essential systems, and also focus on trying to restore and charge up the systems to 80–90% in preparation for the overcast days. It became a key daily chore to monitor and manage the power systems with meticulous strategic detail.

To stop it really getting to me with how frustrating it was, I turned it into a daily game where I challenged myself to see how I could become more and more efficient. I brought cloud cover into my weather forecast two days ahead, so I could manage the solar charging in advance – otherwise a few consecutive days of severe cloud cover could translate into no water. Simple.

It's about always being five steps ahead, having the foresight and planning and taking action ahead of what's coming. Especially when it comes to fundamentals like having water to drink, and a backup in case you're not able to make it for multiple days. My 50 liters of emergency backup water also doubled as ballast. Everything had dual function on this expedition.

I took rehydrate sachets daily with my water, to replace salts and electrolytes that get depleted paddling. I also had two different special hydration mixes. One was a basic hydration race mix for paddling during the day, an isotonic powder with key salts and endurance ingredients. The other was a pea protein recovery mix for after each shift. I'd been using that hydration plan for years, across all world records and adventures, and it works a charm. Hydration is everything, and backing it up with a good meal plan is key.

I would definitely change a great deal on the food side for my next project, but from the hydration side and supplementary bars, I wouldn't change a thing.

Well, there is just one thing: the coffee, my special super treat, my helpful superpower that keeps me going, day or night, rain or shine. I took enough little sachets of coffee to last me 120 days just in case! I could run out of food, but there was no way I was going to run out of coffee, that was for sure.

One of my special items I brought along was a Bodum coffee plunger and some real (not instant) coffee. But I wasn't allowed to use it until the halfway mark. After that, my gift to myself was fresh coffee for the rest of my journey.

I told myself that the only reason I would ever trigger the EPIRB (Emergency Position Indicating Radio Beacon) was if I ran out of coffee!

# Gratitude Attitude

Atlantic Ocean | 18°31'25.56"N 47°51'48.10"W

*'I wept when I had no shoes, until I saw the man begging, who had no feet!'* – Unknown

I need to take a step back here and remind all of you – and myself – to adopt an attitude of gratitude, which is all too easy to forget, both when things are going well, and even more so when they feel like they are not so great.

When I think of complaining about the same freeze-dried meals I had to eat every day, and I was having a bad day, with all the challenges out there, I quickly catch myself and remind myself of how fortunate I really am, just to be able to have 2–3 meals per day – even if they are the same thing for the better part of three months.

Here's a startling statistic that never fails to put it all in perspective for me. Think about this as you leave work today (a job that pays you money) and you're not walking but driving, transporting or cycling home (where there is food in the fridge) and you stop off to buy a couple items from the shop (with money from your bank account or wallet).

If you could shrink the world's population into one small village consisting of only 100 people, where the ratios still represent the total, this is what you would get:

Eighty of those people would live in sub-standard housing. Seventy of those people would be unable to read. Fifty of those people would be suffering from malnutrition – that's half! Only one would have a college education. Only one would have a computer!

the table, a roof over your head and a place to sleep in peace, you are doing better than 75% of people on this planet!

If you have any money in the bank or spare change in your wallet, you are among the top 8% of the wealthiest people in the world. If you woke up this morning with your health and no major illness in your life, then you are more blessed than more than 1 million people out there today that will not survive this week due to illness, malnutrition or starvation.

So, if you are one of those that have all of this, and friends and family that care about you – be very thankful and grateful. And also just stop and take a moment to think about this for a second: maybe we all need to be a little more grateful and appreciate what we have, what we often take for granted, be more present, because it is a gift, that is why it's called the present!

I'm as guilty as the next person when it comes to bitching and complaining about many little things, which in the greater scheme of things are so irrelevant.

I try to remind myself each and every day, as I wake up, just how good I actually have it, even when it really doesn't feel that way. Give a little more, complain a little less and just adopt an attitude of gratitude. You will be amazed how much better it makes you feel.

I believe we all need to remind ourselves constantly how much we all have to be thankful for.

I try and do this weekly out of principle, and I have done it for years. Why? Because I can, and it's the right thing to do. Every little act, no matter how small, actually does make a massive difference to the people you're helping, even if you might not realize it.

My mantra on this I try and live by: be a better human, each and every day in some small way.

If we all do that, we make the world a better place. Compassion, humility and gratitude are three of the most important character traits for human enlightenment. Practicing them will leave a positive impact – it is so very easy to give someone the gift of hope, make someone smile and change their day for the better. It doesn't cost you anything and it's been scientifically proven to be good for you too. It's that simple!

# Trades!

Atlantic Ocean | 18°51'56.65"N 49°8'0.25"W

I felt profoundly grateful as I moved into my 44th day out at sea, alone on the *ImpiFish*. The weather, wind, temperature and conditions were improving all the time as I got further south and west, and I was finally getting into the trade winds. Yeeeehaa! I never thought the day would come. I had finally reached the place I'd wanted to be right from the beginning. It had often seemed like I would never get to this day.

Of course the good spell didn't last long, as they rarely do out here, and things got pretty intense quickly, for a few days of hardcore conditions. General trade winds are 10–20 kn, these conditions were a lot more intense. The wind was full-on and non-stop, 20–25 kn, meaning with 30 kn plus gusts, three-meter seas with 8–12 ft breaking waves all over the place, right through the day and nighttime too, which is sort of the top end of the spectrum of what my little craft and I could handle for more than a couple days in a row. I was still paddling and trying not to have to go onto the para-anchor and slow down; it was tough on all the craft systems, the power resources, and me.

The deck was also constantly submerged under waves and water, which meant I was always wet. I also had a feeling that those deck hatches were still taking in water, which started to really freak me out and play on my mind constantly.

Besides taking its toll on me physically and mentally, the autopilot kept going down as it couldn't handle constant movement of the stern, and the batteries weren't able to handle the load on the system for more than a couple hours in those conditions. My watermaker stopped working, as the seas were too rough. As for the nights – oh my god, the nights became so ridiculously long, and super intense, with little to no sleep at all, which in turn affects EVERYTHING!

Imagine spending a night at sea, alone in a storm, in a capsule size box barely as wide as your shoulders, with little to no air inside this little damp, wet and cold space, because you've locked yourself in and closed all the air vents. The waves knocking you sideways and almost upside down every 10 minutes, you're not sure if the capsule can sustain the beating all night long, and you are alone. You also know the craft you're in has a slow leak and you are thousands of miles from anyone who can possibly help you, and you still have another 10 hours of this until daylight – oh, and then you still have to go out into the conditions described in the pitch black, get cold and wet again and paddle for four hours, not just once, but twice, all before the sun comes up. And then do it all over again, the next night and then the next and the next and the next.

When I'm up there on deck, just trying to stay upright and not get knocked overboard is hard enough, let alone actually continuing to paddle forward. It's almost as hectic as when I'm in my little cabin getting bashed around by the waves hitting side-on, which happened a lot when the autopilot went off, which seemed like most of the time now. Sometimes I could get it working for an hour or two, but rarely.

But like always, with the heavy weather these storms can't last forever and I just kept reminding myself, this too shall pass, this too shall pass! *Hang in there bud, you got this, you can do it. One day at a time, one night at a time, one shift at a time, one hour at a time, one stroke at a time and I will get there. As long as I keep on getting back up and keep moving forward, I will get through this, no matter what it takes!*

And then finally, I hit a significant milestone – the halfway point! Oh yeah! It's important to celebrate the small things, but definitely scream, shout and dance a little for the big things, to remind yourself how far you have come. So that's exactly what I did.

I knew that every stroke I took from now on, no matter how little or far I travelled each day, would bring me closer to getting to the finish line in the Caribbean and the other side of the Atlantic! At 798 NM (1477 km) from the most western point of the African coastline, I was now officially closer to the Americas than Africa, which felt HUGE.

People say don't look backwards, because you're not going that way. Generally I agree with that. Of course you need to focus on what's in front of you, but I also believe that sometimes it's really important to look back, for two reasons. Firstly, to remind yourself of the lessons you've learned along your journey, to help you make better decisions moving forward, and secondly, to remind you how far you have come and what you have accomplished already. This gives you the pride, courage and confidence to know that you can succeed, because of how far you have come and the challenges you've already overcome getting to this point, so now you know you can go the distance and get through the rest of the journey.

When I crossed over the Tropic of Cancer, on a beautiful full moon night on 12 January, I distinctly remember a really positive mental shift. As a Cancerian (aka 'The Crab Man' or 'Captain Crabstick') I am often dramatically affected by the ocean and moon; that night I became acutely aware of what I had been through and survived. Sometimes looking back to move forward is essential for your sanity, mental health, motivation and success. I realized that, having survived everything I had and still moving forward, I could deal with pretty much anything to come – especially since the second half of my journey was meant to be mellower in the trades. I remember feeling instantly more upbeat and more confident when I put it all in perspective.

# Crooked Smile Reroute

Atlantic Ocean | 19°7'43.67"N 50°0'59.58"W

I was still being adversely affected by a low-pressure system wreaking havoc in the North Atlantic, but I was now officially in the trades, even though they were not yet really what they were supposed to be – namely clear blue skies and light, consistent winds behind me. I knew it was going to get better in the days to come, so I just needed to stay mentally strong and weather the next 72 hours, cranking out my daily mileage.

A month earlier, my daily average 24-hour run was roughly 24–28 NM; now I was already starting to average almost 40 NM (75 km) per day! I aimed to increase that to over 40 NM daily over the next couple weeks, when the breeze started settling down a little. With more consistent conditions I knew I would be able to add another daily shift in again too.

I had an awesome day and night during which I unofficially broke Bart de Zwart's solo, 24-hour open ocean (more than 15 miles offshore) unsupported and unassisted world record of just under 50 NM, which he set in 2014, off Tahiti. Then on January 26, I cracked 54 NM over a 24-hour period on my tracker, but I planned to try again in a few weeks' time when I got deeper into the trades, when the *ImpiFish* would be even lighter.

At this point Leven and I came to an important decision. When we looked back from halfway we realized that I'd been pushed really far south from my original course for Florida. The weather had been so consistently challenging – an anomaly, based on the research and data from the last 50 years – so it just made more sense, in order to finish successfully, to aim for Antigua in the Caribbean, like most other transatlantic crossings do from the Canaries. There's a good reason why they do that, because all the trades are generally going that way.

My journey would still be 650 miles more than the average transatlantic crossing, because I started in Agadir rather than the Canaries, and I'd already exceeded the expectations of pretty much everyone on the planet to get this far. So it just became a very simple equation. The amended route meant we would end up with a little bit of a crooked smile, rather than the perfect smile across the Atlantic that I had hoped for. But Operation Smile was the main reason why we were doing this. So actually in hindsight, everything worked out exactly the way it should, as I was mending those crooked smiles through this journey.

When you look back in hindsight, it seems serendipitous, as plans tend to work out just the way they're meant to. They worked out that way for me, and for the beautiful crooked smiles we fixed on all the little kids' faces.

# Catching Monkeys!

Atlantic Ocean | 18°56'34.18"N 51°29'53.30"W

I was now 52 days into my epic adventure, almost two months alone at sea on the *ImpiFish* since leaving Morocco on 6 December 2016. I had paddled just over 1,2 million strokes – 1,235,520 to be exact, @ 36s/pm, according to my Garmin Fenix. I was 965 NM (17,880 km) from the most western tip of Africa, and exactly due north of South America!

In the clear-weather time ahead I hoped to finally be able to check and re-seal the leaking hatches again. I was certain I was going to find some water; now it was a matter of just how to manage the slow leaks weekly and the power and system issues moving forward.

The only way I could stop from getting really stressed and negative from the challenges was to treat them as a daily game to get better and more efficient at. So my daily aim was to create a manageable, barebones safe structure: make a minimum of five liters of water per day, if possible, and still have enough battery left to run the autopilot as much as I could, even if this was only for an hour or two, while still being able to use the chartplotter for half the day and intermittently at night, to manage routing, course, corrections, direction and distance, and to be picked up on radar at night by passing ships. If I had any extra I would use this to charge my phones and GoPros, which were all luxury devices in the greater scheme of things.

This was no simple or easy feat, but as a sailor I always enjoyed the navigation aspect, so I learned to have fun with it. I tweaked my course daily according to the cloud cover and forecasted weather; figuring it all out was fascinating, and super rewarding when I got it right.

I spent a day moving the last of my food rations forward from the back two leaky deck hatch compartments, to underneath my sleeping space. I couldn't afford any more food losses. I sponged out just three liters of water, which wasn't as bad as I thought it was going to be; that meant that the fixing and sealing I had done previously had actually worked, so I was more stoked than you can imagine!

I moved all the remaining food under my mattress, which was the safest place I knew. It forced me to try and eat more too, which I needed to do, as I was becoming one very skinny little sea pirate! Plus sleeping became even more uncomfortable which was good – it forced me out of my cabin! Sleeping more wouldn't get me across the ocean, only paddling would!

I'd developed some clever mental-deception tricks to help me get through a great deal of my challenges. One was to set bite-sized goals and then make mini goals within those goals, with each one having a mini treat, to positively reward myself for achieving them. It's my way of distracting myself from the big picture, when it feels too over-whelming for the mind to handle. It simplifies everything and keeps it all manageable, keeps me focused and keeps me motivated and moving forward.

One of those strategies was tracking my 'golden monkeys' from the Talisker rowboat race. Every weather update I had with Leven, he let me know how much closer I was getting and what distance I still had to catch them up in order to pass the last back monkey. Finally, 52 days into my journey, he told me I had not only caught up to one of the row-boats, but I had actually OVERTAKEN two of them! I was super stoked!

That night I rewarded myself with a very special milestone celebration: a big-size Bar One chocolate. I turned the light down low, put on some nice slow music, got into my only dry pair of soft cotton pants and savored that chocolate bar, one slow incredible tasty bite at a time. Then I did a little dance on the deck of the *ImpiFish* and laughed hysterically, like a madman. A perfect example of positive mental distraction at its finest.

I know it sounds crazy, but it felt like winning gold at the Olympics, or winning the biggest pitch for a dream job, or client, like reaching the summit of Everest, but bigger... That milestone was huge, as I realized now I was fast, faster than I should have been at my size, on my tiny little *ImpiFish*... and I was getting even lighter and faster by the day now! It was a game changer for me and the confirmation of what I was doing was pretty extraordinary.

I was now paddling even faster than I thought we could go, especially if I was outpacing the rowboats, which was simply incredible! I was not only catching up to them, but actually overtaking them!

I couldn't rest on my laurels for long though – I still had my next four mental milestones to chase and I was about to reach the next one.

# Following Venus

Atlantic Ocean | 19°4'57.44"N 52°8'50.19"W

Passing the 34°W mark on the chart meant I was exactly due north of the most eastern point of South America. From that day onward I would be traveling along the top western part of the South American coast, all the way across the second half of the Atlantic crossing, till I hit the Caribbean. I made a rough estimate that I had 40 days to go to the finish.

It was as if the ocean itself offered me a reward for that milestone, and it came in the form of my first super flying fish! It was another sure sign that I was officially in the trades, with a forecast of five straight days of the perfect wind, pure ENE! Pure joy!

I was now the most remote I could possibly be on the planet. I was over 1750 km from anyone and anywhere in the world, literally in the middle of the Atlantic, and completely out of range of any rescue aircraft and as far away from help or any other human as I could possibly be – I was actually closer to the astronauts on the International Space Station than I was to any humans on land, and that, my friends is pretty damn remote! I should have been the most worried and concerned, but instead I felt more calm, connected, in tune, happy, inspired, confident, comfortable, content and free than I have been in as long as I can remember. That was an incredible feeling, out there alone in literally the middle of the Big Blue Atlantic Ocean. It was simply perfect.

Connecting to nature in its most raw, peaceful and pure state, connecting directly to the source, is incredibly powerful. The transfer of energy, while following your passion and living your life's purpose, is like tapping into your superpower, your greatest self, fueled with a positivity that cannot be contained and just simply wants to burst out. Your whole body and mind is alive and overflowing with positive energy, as if you have a battery pack that just never runs flat. It's like discovering the fountain of youth!

I don't think very much in life comes close to this; if I could bottle it and create the recipe for it, I would never have to work again... but I do think the secret to finding it is to follow your passions and your bliss and this in turn will lead you to your life's purpose, your reason for being – what the Japanese call 'ikigai'.

That night while resting, on a short paddle break, sitting on my little deck at 1:30 am, I found myself in awe, transfixed, literally lost in space, looking up into the deep, dark pin-holed starry sky, a speckled canvas glistening and twinkling all around me. This is a universe you don't normally see with the naked eye. All the stars and the entire galaxy and Milky Way were so bright and ablaze with detail, it was simply mesmerizing. I let myself go completely and become immersed, surrounded by the deep magic of the ocean and enveloped by the magnificence of the night sky. A night and moment in time I will never forget and that's deeply etched into mind and soul forever!

With no moon at all, Venus shone so bright it left its own signature, a dancing light trail along the ocean surface for me to follow while paddling, guiding me west. I felt like I was following a magic treasure map, a map meant only for me, that only I could decipher.

*A fairy dust trail on the water, to help me find my way home...*

There's magic out here, an energy and pulse in the ocean, nature's pulse, its heart beating. It's so immense, all consuming, it is part of us, but you have to let go, be in flow, be still, in order to hear it; listen closely, as it runs so deep.

*Where else would you want to be on the planet, than right here, right now, when you have all this?* I found the answer immediately within. *Right here, right now, absorbed and immersed in every droplet, every shadow, every sight, every sound, every twinkle, every shooting star, right here in this very moment!* Pure bliss.

I felt the Caribbean calling me, the sea was in my veins and the islands in my bones. I could hear Captain Jack Sparrow and the Black Pearl beckoning me and my trusty *ImpiFish*… I could almost smell the crisp, salty island air and taste that nice cold Caribbean rum awaiting me just over a month away. *It's coming soon my friend… but not yet, not just yet.*

Now I just needed to focus. Day by day, shift by shift, hour by hour, stroke by stroke, always reminding myself constantly of my 'why'. Visualize, breathe, manage and maintain the systems. Feel the rhythm, feel the ride, feel the ocean, flow with it, slide and glide – but don't get complacent. Safety first; I needed to keep to my routine, stay vigilant, not get sloppy, and always 'beware' that fat lady, who still hadn't sung. *You still have a long way to go, Bertish.*

# Quicksand and the Sea Chameleon

Atlantic Ocean | 18°48'22.57"N 53°26'1.70"W

The next four days leading into February were super intense, with the weather intensifying beyond what the forecasts had predicted, yet again – and things were only going to get even more hardcore before they let up in five days' time.

The weather went from being beautiful and sunny with light trade wind conditions through Sunday, when I was suddenly rocked by an adverse surface current in the water, which was almost one knot in strength. It took me backwards and slowed me to less than half of my daily speed and distance – but that wasn't the main challenge. The challenge was that it was flowing in exactly the opposite direction to the wind and direction I was trying to paddle, so it made for really rough, choppy water and confused seas.

Any time I took a break from paddling, which I had to do pretty regularly, as every stroke was putting almost double the load on my body, I just went backwards… and what made it even more challenging and frustrating was this wasn't just for a couple hours, this was for a full two days; 48 hours getting pushed backward and north while I was doing everything in my power to go the other direction!

It was the most frustrating thing I have ever experienced. I paddled 16 hours that first day, and every stroke felt like I was caught in quicksand; like I was paddling through mercury, everything felt super slow and heavy.

I was straining against every stroke, every hour breaking me down. Every break I took to rehydrate and reenergize I watched the tracker going backwards almost a mile every hour. It was soul destroying as well as physically and mentally draining, and by 10 pm that night I was completely broken. Every muscle and bone ached from strain, the over exertion, the fatigue. *No more, I need a proper break.*

The next day was the same, except I approached it with a new game plan. I did the best I could and broke my shifts down into shorter, bite-size, two-hour blocks. To soften the load on my body, I changed to the smallest blade I had, with the shortest paddle shaft and the one with the most flex in the shaft, so it had less power and would absorb more of the load and not transfer it onto my body. That morning before starting my 5 am shift I focused on making peace with letting go of what I couldn't control, taking it slow and easy. *You can fight the ocean, but you will always lose... Play the game, it's a marathon, not a sprint,* I reminded myself.

I knew the conditions would turn to my favor again within the next 36 hours; these surface currents generally don't last more than 48 hours, or 50 miles across max, so I knew I would slowly but surely get through it. It wasn't worth destroying myself for the sake of 40 miles. *Let it go, don't fight it, breathe, slow it down, relax...*

I turned the chartplotter off so I couldn't see the numbers – watching them going backwards was killing me, it was simply better not to know – and just get on with it.

The next day the adverse current eased. The wind was supposed to drop into a soft and relaxing 10–15 knots of steady following breeze. I thought I would have time to write my blog and connect with everyone... but no such luck.

*So much for that forecast.* I started getting hammered by 18–25 kn, sometimes more, day and night. The confused seas made it even more hectic and intense. And the forecast of 20 kn-plus went right through till the 4th of February. What a nightmare!

All the systems were strained when the seas got to three meters plus, with over 20 kn of breeze, because when it's like this the stronger gusts are 25–30 kn, which makes for some nasty breaking seas.

The autohelm failed a great deal of the time. I had burnt two of these rams out completely now, they were completely fried... Now I was on the third, meaning I only had one backup left and that one was only working in short bursts.

So when the autohelm goes down, which is a lot, I had to get up, no matter whether I was on shift, resting, sleeping, making food, in my clothes in my cabin or suited up on deck, in the daytime or in the middle of the night. I'd have to get up to take over, otherwise it would lock itself off to one side, which would turn me broadside – side-on to the conditions, which is super dangerous and becomes wet and wild quickly. I either had to go out there and take over, or go on the sea anchor, which is something I was trying to avoid because it would stop me almost dead in my tracks and I would lose so many more miles – and I would be getting battered by the elements all going in the same direction.

Safety becomes paramount in those conditions. Cooking was dangerous as I was constantly getting battered and rolled around. The watermaker also battled to work, so I had to start using my emergency water – I reckoned I was more than halfway across, so I could get away with it. In these conditions I was tethered at all times, connected to my harness almost 24/7 and wearing my big wave surf leash most of the time now.

Any split second I was out of my hatch, I'd shut it using both locks immediately behind me. It was absolutely vital to be vigilant on this; let your guard down and slip just once, just for two seconds, and BAM – a rogue wave could get you, flood the cabin and fry all the electronics, navigational and safety equipment, and/or it would knock me overboard... either way, it would be game over, the end! It was that simple.

Rogue waves happened out there all the time, every day, and it only takes one. Some are small, 4–5 feet, some 8–10 feet and bigger. Even though I was very aware of it, it was so easy to get caught off guard. It almost happened numerous times – once, while on the satellite phone, which I managed to keep hold of and not drop into the deep – and whenever it happened I was fatigued; that's when mistakes happen.

I tried to focus on the positives each and every day to keep my head up and stay positive with good music, and some good audio books. I just had to keep it all together, physically and even more so mentally, which is toughest during the very long nights, getting battered from all sides.

Maybe these conditions were also a good distraction for me mentally, to get me through to the next milestone: the 6th Feb marked 60 days at sea, with 30 more to go!

My aim every day was to just concentrate on what was right in front of me, allow myself to get lost in the now, immerse myself in every action, and let nothing else enter my mind.

I focused on any and all the silly little positive things that happened daily, anything that gave me an excuse to laugh or smile and have some fun, no matter how small. One time I found a little baby squid I called Squirt on the deck, another time it was a little sea-louse. I'd see an unknown little creature getting caught by a wave, laugh and smile and wish it on its way. So take whatever opportunities you can to love, laugh and smile… because things can always be worse!

It is super important to embrace every chance to laugh because it really positively changes your mental state and your chemistry in your body when you laugh and smile. Even if you have to force it. Fake it till you become it, if you have to, whatever it takes!

So no matter what the conditions, I made myself smile, then put my head down and just took one stroke at a time, one hour at a time, one shift at a time, one day at a time. Sometimes you just have to grind it out… head down and just grind it out, that's just part of the process.

I visualized becoming a sea chameleon; to be flexible, adapt, morph and change myself to be my environment. I didn't just want to survive it, I wanted to thrive through it and become its fluid counterpart. *Become like water my friend* – as Bruce Lee said. Keep evolving with it, learning, growing and moving forward with it. Just become it.

# Full Throttle

As the sun went down the last light caught the white caps of the four-meter waves breaking all around me in a heaving ocean in motion. The wind howled through the evening light, gusting between 25 and 30 kn.

I'd been at sea for 62 days and had less than a month to go.

I cringed at the thought of yet another night of this. After five nights in my little cabin in the pitch black being pounded by these seas, I was exhausted, burnt out, depleted. I was running on pure adrenalin, after another 15-hour day. There was no other choice; there was no end to this turmoil in sight.

Every night in these conditions seemed like the longest 12 hours of my life. I knew I just had to get through this night first, that was goal number one; then I needed to copy and paste that, physically and mentally endure it all over again for the next night, and as many nights that followed, until the weather broke.

Just when you think it can't get worse out here, it does.

I was taking a quick break, after being on shift for a full 12 hours. I had literally just finished making my little freeze-dried food meal in my tiny cabin. I'd changed into dry clothes and sat back, ready to take a well-deserved rest. I breathed out a deep sigh… *ahhhh…* and that's when I heard it: *BAH!* The sound of my autopilot ram burning out and melting into itself, literally an hour after I had replaced the old one.

This was the third and last backup ram I had. Somehow I had miraculously managed to recalibrate it and get it working, and now this, in these conditions, with massive breaking waves and squalls all around me. Words cannot really describe the intensity of what that means.

I jumped into my damp boardies, clipped into my harness and quickly went back outside to release the pilot from the steering mechanism and free the rudder. As I looked up into the creeping darkness, a wave broke right over me, knocking me off balance and almost tossing me over the side; but I was holding on tight on multiple points, and just managed to shut the hatch before my cabin got swamped.

It was too dangerous to be outside on deck at night in these conditions, even clipped in, but there was simply no other option.

I set the steering at 10 degrees to starboard and locked it off to hold me drifting slightly side-on in one direction, then retreated back to my cabin, now sopping wet, to reassess. I knew what I had just done and what was about to happen for the next 12 very long hours.

Without the autohelm keeping me going downwind with it, I would have to drift side-on, 45–60 degrees to the wind and weather all night long. This meant I was going to get continually hit by these huge breaking crests, side-on and possibly rolled. I was just going to have to deal with it, one hour at a time to get through this night.

*BOOM!* I didn't even have time to brace for impact; I was flung across my cabin, hitting the opposite wall hard. The *ImpiFish* shook and shuddered.

I was over 1500 km out in the middle of the Atlantic, alone at night, in weather to be afraid of… and this was just the beginning. It was the first five minutes of the longest 72 hours of my life!

For the next 12 hours I was on high alert, listening intently to every sound in my surroundings. My mind automatically assessed every wave rumbling by, calculating the direction, the distance, the percentage ratio of the next one, and then bracing for impact as it hit me side-on. Was I going to slide sideways in my little craft, or get rolled over and inverted? Would my little *ImpiFish* handle the battering through the night, or would it start to delaminate and fall apart, thousands of miles from any other help or humans or land?

By midnight I felt like it was too dangerous to be side-on through the rest of the night as the *ImpiFish* and I were getting beaten up and rolled around too much. Leven and I agreed that taking out the centerboard was the next best option, during these heavy conditions, as I couldn't afford the *ImpiFish* getting badly damaged from the continuous side-on pounding from the waves, with autopilot not working while I was in the cabin trying to get some rest.

After removing the centerboard and keeping it next to me in my cabin through the night, when we got hit by a wave the *ImpiFish* still got knocked sideways, but instead of getting knocked over, rolling or getting semi-inverted (which is always scary) now she slid sideways across the water and didn't get as hammered and battered by every wave as before.

I had to stay super low in my cabin at all times now; to keep my center of gravity as low as possible, because without the centerboard, my little craft was super unstable and could flip and invert much more easily, but whatever you have to do to survive and get you and your little craft through till the morning in one piece, safely so you can continue on, then that's what you do. It's that simple!

Every minute is so intense when you're running on high alert; anxiety, stress and adrenalin. By the time morning broke I was physically, mentally and emotionally drained. I looked outside and my heart sank; it looked exactly the same as the day before. Then the forecast came through from Leven on the satellite phone. 'More of the same Captain, but it should ease up a bit tomorrow, but you'll handle it, because you're strong as steel!'

*You can do this, Bertish, you can do this!* I tell myself. *Only one more night to endure...*

I had started talking to myself out loud a lot. Positive self-talk and affirmations helped me stay in the present and deal with what was in front of me without getting negative or overwhelmed.

The forecast of super-light conditions for the next day turned out to be optimistic; I would still have 15–20 kn for another week, but I wasn't going to complain – 15–20 kn is a whole lot better than 25 kn-plus, and the sea state dropped from 4,5 meters to 2,5 meters, which just about made everything manageable – just.

179

That next day I even managed to get the *ImpiFish* surfing a couple times, but it gets really sketchy and out of control and I almost broached twice, so I kept that to a minimum. *Safety first, just get to the other side in one piece Bertish. You have a lot of little faces relying on you...*

I'd strained a ligament opening one of the super tight hatches, but that was the least of my challenges. I also seemed to have pulled a muscle in my left arm bicep; when the pain kept growing in my left shoulder, I realized that it was actually my rotator cuff, starting to become an issue.

I had cuts all over me, and a cooking burn on my arm from when the stove spilled boiling water on me after we got hit by a wave. I had to manage all these cuts and scrapes to ensure they didn't all go infected; even though I treated them, they were constantly wet, and with my immune system being at an all-time low from the endless exertion and not ever getting more than two hours' sleep through the night, they were battling to heal.

After the op on my right shoulder six months before I started this project, the surgeon told me it would be three or four years before I would need to get the other shoulder done. Of course I forgot to mention I'd be doing 1,5 million shoulder rotations within the coming months, which would kind of speed up that process!

I called my good friend Dr Lynnelle Hoeks on the satellite phone at a time I knew she'd be awake and asked for some advice. 'Anti-inflammatories and try not to paddle much for a while, if that's possible!' Easier said than done. She was right and I knew it, but how else was I going to get across this ocean?

I went through the extensive first aid kit I had prepped with her before leaving. I counted out my painkillers and anti-inflammatories; I had enough of the latter to get me to the other side, and the pain was something I could just mentally work through as it built over the next 29 days. The problem was the anti-inflammatories that I took that day messed with my balance, which is not the thing you really want to find out while paddling for 12 hours day or night. That was pretty much the last thing I needed right now. *But hey, it's character building right!* I said to myself. Then laughed out loud. It was funny, sort of.

After the weather eased a little, I tried to take one full day off, to just stay in my cabin and give my body a break, slow things down; hydrate properly, catch up on sleep, take lots of vitamins and boosters for my immune system, and nurse all my wounds properly – a couple of them were looking questionable and I had to focus on keeping them dry and looking after them properly, even if only for just one day. I also wanted to find solutions to some of the challenges, like figuring out a new drogue system for intense conditions like I'd just had.

My South African flag had been ripped to smithereens by the intense winds and I got hit by a rogue wave that swamped me and everything on deck, washing my water bottle, sunscreen and toothbrush overboard – all gone. I watched the red top of my Enduren water bottle floating away and there was nothing I could do. It was just 20 feet away, but in 20kn of breeze if I'm separated from my craft for more than 10 seconds, I'm dead. So bye-bye, last water bottle! This might not sound like a major issue, but I only had one extra bottle that I used to pee in at night, for safety reasons, so I wouldn't have to go on deck.

Now I would just have to drink out of that. Sanitary concerns go out the window pretty quickly when you're fighting for survival!

Almost worse, later that day a rogue wave took my paddle straight off the deck while I was sorting out the autopilot. The paddle was locked into its normal place, but just got hit at a weird angle and – BOOM – it popped out of its safety bracket and was gone overboard in a split second. I remember seeing something flash past me, out the corner of my eye, but by the time I'd closed the hatch and looked up, my paddle was 4 feet off the side of the *ImpiFish*. I didn't even blink, knowing I was tethered into my harness. I took a huge leap of faith, grabbed my harness tether in one hand as a backup safety and dived over the side with my arm stretched out as far as possible, like Spider-Man swinging from his web. The tether engaged at 5 meters, the *ImpiFish* lurched to the side and – direct hit, *I got ya!* A millisecond later and it would have been gone.

Everything happens very quickly out there, in split seconds, so you better learn to embrace change, or you are done for.

It's like life on steroids, moving at full tilt with no down time or intermission – and when the lights go out it's still going full tilt, so suck it up, buttercup, get used to it cause the only thing guaranteed out there is that it's going to be totally different in a couple of hours – and that's true for every day, all day, all night, all the time. This was my new norm.

# Being like Water

As the sun came out for the first time in three days, I resolved to stay low, slow, smooth and just flow.

The long-range forecast was looking more positive, which was great news. I would be getting some solid miles in over the next week, to get me closer to the finish line. *Less than 30 days and counting!*

I hadn't used the autopilot in five days now, but with milder conditions I hoped it would handle everything better, at least for a little while.

My new drogue downwind systems seemed to work far better than what I'd been recommended to bring with me. I spent my nights working out the angles and playing with the drift vectors, to wiggle my way down my course and still stay roughly on track. It was pretty fascinating and I learned a great deal, very quickly, because I had to.

It was a great mental challenge, working with the drogue system as my steering assist, for when my autopilot went out, and when the wind got really strong. It definitely slowed me down and was not efficient, but it was the best I could do with what I had. *Remember, I'm solo and it's a marathon not a sprint.*

I was amazed at how effective I could get the drift angles, even without any sails, locking off my steering angles by 30 degrees, one side for 3 hours and then changing it to the other side 3 hours later, so I would zig-zag down the route, as I had to get really creative. I was even impressed with myself. *Damn, you got some skills son! That's seriously impressive improv drogue navigation!*

There is always another way – even if it may not be pretty, or perfect! It was crucially important to mentally and physically slow it all down, focus on not fighting the elements and start to learn to flow with everything more.

I've always believed sleep, rest, recovery, exercise and nature are the best solutions to solve difficult challenges in life. Right now I didn't need more exercise or nature; I needed rest. Sometimes you just need to be able to step back from it all, get a different perspective. Slow it all down, stop, breathe… close your eyes and sleep. A rested mind brings new perspectives, a positive attitude and fresh solutions.

There's always more than one way to get through anything. To solve any challenge, any situation, get some rest, because when you're tired and drained, you don't think clearly, and it affects everything. It's always harder to see the positive in the negative when you are tired. Your brain needs to rest, reboot, reset so it can move forward again more efficiently.

*Just flow with it and don't fight it! Use and embrace the path of least resistance.*

I had to constantly remind myself to slow it down. This was a 90-day-plus marathon. I had to manage myself, the weather, the navigation and the systems as best I could all the time, with better strategies to give me the long-term result I was looking for: to finish this alive, in one piece, bring smiles to the faces of thousands of kids, and hopefully inspire many people along the way.

How do you eat an elephant? One bite at a time. I was breaking everything down into bite-sized, more manageable chunks in order to keep my focus and motivation high until the end. This was no longer just a monumental SUP project, raising money for charities; it had become a whole lot more.

It took me just over 60 days before I became one with the *ImpiFish* and my blue world. I surrendered and merged into the flow of the ocean and became one with the elements, shifted my attitude, let go and slipped in sync with the source. From that point on, I was in flow, in the most pure and primal form and at one with everything. I lost all sense of going against the elements, just an immense sense of love, appreciation and gratitude, in awe of this environment in which I was completely immersed and at one with the blue that surrounded me.

I became the wind, the waves, the sky, the sea, at one with the creatures, the storms and all that is the ocean. The ocean became me and I became the sea!

I was comfortable and at one, in the most pure sense, with nature; truly free, humbled, grounded, content. Once I let go and surrendered into the flow, I became part of it. I was it, I was flow, I was truly free, I was home!

I dug in my paddle and moved forward. It was going to be an awesome day. How did I know? Because I chose it to be, and would make it so. I was in the flow.

*Caribbean, here I come...*

# A Not-so-Friendly Visitor from the Deep!

Atlantic Ocean | 18°39'47.60"N 56°23'46.03"W

For the first time in almost three weeks, the wind was lighter and more manageable, in the 15-kn range. The sea state calmed down dramatically and the sun even came back out, with some beautiful blue skies for the sunrise. I felt like I could finally start enjoying the last part of this journey, instead of just trying to survive it.

I'd been on shift paddling for just over an hour when I got really hot, so did my usual quick 30-second dip overboard to cool down and to rinse off. I could only do this when the weather was mild, but it was something I tried to do whenever I could.

I jumped back on deck to set up the watermaker to make my daily five-liter water ration since the sun was out, and my batteries were almost fully charged. I was sitting on deck, leaning forward holding the steering system – I'd switched the autopilot off so I had enough power for the watermaker. While I was watching my water bottle slowly filling, drip by precious drip, protective as a mother hen looking after her chicks, I suddenly had a weird premonition.

I glanced up and something caught my eye, just over my shoulder. Everything went into slow motion, and then BAAM! It hit us from below and ricocheted off the side of the stern of the *ImpiFish*. Out of the corner of my eye I saw a very large dark shape heading up towards the stern, at speed. The moment of impact happened quickly, hitting the side and underneath of the *ImpiFish* so hard it almost knocked me overboard. I held on tight to the side of the craft, as she rolled sideways and I pulled hard on my steering lines to regain my balance, as the thing deflected away. As it veered off its head broke the surface and I was looking almost directly into a big black eye, before it submerged quickly and went under the *ImpiFish*! I knew instantly exactly what it was: a really large Great White shark!

I could see her crystal-clear. Big and dark and fat, with that opaque black eye looking right at me as she swam off to the starboard side, a sleek, smooth hunting machine. She swished forcefully off and swam away about 20 meters, with her dorsal fin now very visible slicing through the water. Then she veered around to come back at me again, moving towards my side like a scud missile. I braced for a mouth and teeth, impact or both, but neither happened. She came close enough I could have reached down to touch her and she slid right underneath me. That's when I saw how wide she was – at least 1,5 meters, which is a lot wider than the *ImpiFish*. That was terrifying in itself, because it meant she was at least as long as us, maybe even a little longer, at close to six meters in length. I knew that mouth and those teeth could do some serious damage and sink me, if she decided to take a bite out of the side of my little craft!

That's when you realize how alone you really are, and how far from help. I went into fight or flight mode, except there was nowhere to go. And I knew she might well be coming back to investigate me as possible lunch!

By this time I had come to my senses. I grabbed up at the console next to me and pulled my deck knife out from its sheath; I was instantly ready for battle, if that's what it was going to take.

She turned to come back for the second round, swimming at me steady, with speed and intention. I was ready for battle with my deck knife. I had no idea what I was going to do, but I was ready! I needed to do whatever it would take to protect myself and my little home, because if that beast took a proper bite out the side of my craft, it would probably flood my watertight compartments and I could sink within minutes…

As she came in for what I thought would be a full-blown attack, I was crouched ready, knife in hand – *pirate ready*! She got within five feet of me, turned sharply with a splash of her tail. She circled around me one last time, keeping eye contact with me the entire time and then disappeared into the deep blue.

I grabbed my GoPro to capture her as she came back again, but obviously she was camera shy, or scared of my technicolored board shorts and pirate beard, because she never came back again, and I was pretty happy about that. I was left fully adrenalized, scared, shaken, wired, stoked and everything else all rolled into one. It took me about 20 minutes to stop shaking and to put down my trusty deck knife!

After researching it further I discovered that it's only the large female Great Whites that follow the migration routes between Africa and the Caribbean. So it's not surprising I got to actually see one – just would have preferred not to have such a close encounter with one as big as this.

I reckon, as it was daylight, with such good water visibility, she was coming from deep for a surprise breaching attack, but at the last moment probably realized I wasn't what she thought. Perhaps she expected a whale calf separated from its mother, and changed her mind, but a shark this size, moving at that speed, can't stop, so when she veered to the side at the last second she still hit me. I wasn't complaining. My rudder wouldn't have taken a direct hit from a shark that size. She was like a small bus with teeth – and no brakes.

Needless to say I didn't swim again that day!

# Situational Assessment

To calm down after my close encounter with the Great White I decided to take stock of everything. Where I was at, what I had lost and what I had left, what to implement and what I would need to ration.

I calculated that I had less than 25 days to go at my current average speed of 40 NM per day. I was three quarters of the way through my journey. I had been at sea alone for 67 days. I had crossed three time zones, averaging 74 km every day. I had covered a total of 4910 km since I left Agadir, and I had 1020 NM / 1930 km left to go to the finish. That meant I was 26 days from Antigua if I covered 40 NM per day, or 23 days and 3 hours at 45 NM per day. My average speed over the entire journey was 1,5 knots – and now I was getting a lot faster!

According to my Garmin Fenix watch, my total number of paddle strokes after 65 days was 1,404,000, at an average rate of 36 strokes per minute, and an average of 10 hours paddled per day, which included the days I was on sea anchor, so it was really more like 12–14 hours.

System problems were under control, but still a constant challenge to manage daily. System challenges included:
- 3 x autopilot rams burnt out and failed; the one left was my old backup, which only worked occasionally, so now I only kept it for very special occasions and used it for short bursts of an hour at a time, because I might really need it at the end. 95% of the time I was now steering with the makeshift system I had developed.
- 2 x steering systems failed – autopilot and my foot-steering system.
- 1 x watermaker constantly needing bleeding.

- 5 x leaks now repaired to the best of my ability and monitored, some daily, some weekly; the hatches were still taking in water, just very slowly now.
- Multiple drogue systems made with lines and bridle systems implemented.
- Multiple new steering systems made and implemented – the one I had now probably worked better and was far more reliable than what was built into the craft from the beginning.

Items lost overboard so far due to rogue waves or being inverted or broaching in heavy weather included:
- 1 x hat
- 1 x sunglasses
- 1 x hatch cover
- 1 x bucket
- 2 x tubes of Island Tribe suntan lotion
- 2 x water bottles
- And many baby biodegradable bamboo wipes – *oh shit!*

Injuries so far:
- 1 x torn shoulder muscle
- 1 x strained finger tendon
- 1 x damaged rotator cuff – now needing surgery when I finish
- Multiple holes in my hands
- Multiple holes in my knee and all over my legs
- Possibly a broken big toe

My nutrition and hydration intake included:
- 40 kg of food
- 5–6 liters water hydration and 1x coffee each day
- 10 kg of mixed nuts
- 5 kg Enduren hydration mix
- 5 kg of Racefood

I had kept all of my rubbish over the last 65 days in an 8-liter dry bag! That's pretty damn good, over two months.

I had taken out a R280,000 (US$20,000) loan against my house to make the project happen, as we were still short at the end of 2016 before starting.

Items left:
- Extra water allowance daily for washing and basic sanitary – still zero!
- Sanity – small traces still remaining, but greater similarities to a rogue sea pirate evident.
- Sense of humor – very little remaining, but building as I got closer to Antigua.
- Stress levels – decreasing daily after storms and hectic weather had subsided.
- 4 x paddles (still have all of them – stoked!)
- 40 liters (from original 60 liters) emergency water still available.
- Clean clothes – none.
- 70 kg of me remaining, after losing at least 10 kg and dropping two sizes.
- 200 g of paddling calluses on my hands.
- 2 x tubes Island Tribe remaining.
- 26 x ration packs remaining – hopefully enough food to get me through the next 25–28 days. (A good incentive to paddle faster!)

I reminded myself that I was pioneering something that no one on earth had ever done before, shifting perceptions of what's possible and redefining the limits of the sport of stand-up paddleboarding, so I really wasn't doing too bad, as there really was no playbook for what I was doing, I was creating it daily.

Best of all, we had raised almost R1 million so far for Signature of Hope Trust, Operation Smile and The Lunchbox Fund, and also raised awareness for the Two Oceans Aquarium in Cape Town, which had integrated my project updates into their ocean educational program and showed my videos to over 50,000 children, focused on ocean conservation and ocean health.

I finished my list in my tiny little cabin. I felt truly blessed, as I watched the sunset to the west, while simultaneously watching the moon rise in the east, on the opposite horizon. *I didn't even know that happened in this amazing world and universe we live in. Wow, mind blowing and awe inspiring. I love nature.*

As I paddled through my last shift that night with the moonlight dancing on the water in front of me, it felt like I had a spirit guide leading me home. I was feeling the presence of some guiding hand and nature strongly and so deeply now more than ever, a powerful energy and source greater than me. I was starting to let go completely, connecting deeply with it in ways I find hard to explain.

# Powered by Nature — and Stripe

Atlantic Ocean | 18°45'2.49"N 57°5'34.99"W

After the Big Fish encounter, all the other fish deserted us, except for Stripe.

Stripe is a pilot fish. He started following me and the *ImpiFish* sometime in January and became a valued member of my team and probably my most loyal friend in my little ocean family. He was the only one not to leave my side through thick and thin, literally always.

Pilot fish generally hang around sharks and turtles for a free lunch, but not often with this sort of craft. When things were calm, I often swam under and next to the *ImpiFish*, hanging underneath and scrubbing off the goose barnacles, which grow on the bottom and slow you down, unless you attend to them. Sometimes I just used to dive down and glide holding onto the rudder, relaxed and content to simply be in flow. I would often find Stripe swimming up next to me, coming right up to my face, so super friendly, tame and comfortable with me.

*Thanks Stripe, for your friendship and loyalty, it shall be rewarded by not being eaten by your friend, the hungry sea pirate, even if I run out of food.*

Everyone needs a travel buddy in life, and the Mighty Stripe was mine. Even with all the big teeth that came knocking, Stripe was brave, bold and fearless and never left my side. I often put on my goggles and popped my head over the side just to check in on him. He would come up inquisitively to say hi and then shoot off again. Every now and again I would see him dart out from under the *ImpiFish* bow, to check out some weed or something floating nearby; then he would quickly dart back under again. Every time I saw him I shouted, *Stripppeee! Go get 'em boy!*

I swam with a couple of very shy dusky dolphins after another awesome sunset shift, and watched in amazement as all the magical colors illuminated the horizon, clouds and evening sky. Later, I did the midnight shift below a canopy of stars, and the light of the full moon and night sky reflected on the almost mirror-like dark ocean canvas.

I took in a few deep breaths of the clean, salty Atlantic Ocean air. I thought I would truly find happiness and fulfillment by reaching the other side, but I now realized I was mistaken; I had just found it, right here, right now, living in the moment out here, under a starry dark night sky.

*Right here, right now, I am home, at peace and completely free.*

The next morning I started my day with a refreshing morning skinny-dip in the big Atlantic blue, always the cure to revitalize and recharge body, mind and soul. There was almost zero breeze, so I had to work hard to pull the *ImpiFish* through the water. Just to paddle one NM/1,8 km took more than an hour. Every stroke with no breeze takes monumental effort, as she was still 700 kg all in, with all my gear and food – and my growing rotator cuff and bicep issues didn't help and neither were getting better.

But then after my swim, I stood there on my little deck, naked, salty, sun kissed and unafraid, dripping with Atlantic blue, body soaking in the morning sunshine, re-energizing my soul. I realized I was similar to a battery pack getting charged by nature! That's all I needed. Charged and powered by nature. It doesn't take much more than that to make me happy.

You really don't need much more than this to be happy in life, it's really that simple. It's life's magic recipe for happiness and the fountain of youth. I just stood there motionless, naked, in awe at the sheer scale of the beauty that surrounded me, calm and still, deafeningly quiet. Even though everything's perfectly calm, somehow the ocean is still in motion and always in flux. A myriad of cross-hatching swells, like a magnificent moving oil canvas painting, unfolding and changing around me as I took it all in. It was mesmerizing and awe-inspiring, the epitome of nature in all her glory and effortless perfection!

Such moments of pure joy, tranquility and bliss are often very short-lived, but I've learned to catch them, slow them down, get totally absorbed in them, savor them, and hold them tight for as long as I can. They are always fleeting and I'm okay with that, because at least I'm one of the lucky few on the planet that get to experience those moments – and they are often quickly replaced by much harder, challenging, darker and difficult times.

One of the challenges I was trying to come to grips with was my beard. I'd never had one up until this project. It was bushy and pirate-like and did a great job protecting my face from the sun, but it was annoying as hell on my face – even more so since I was sleep deprived and physically depleted most of the time. I wouldn't be able to do anything about that damn fur until I got to the other side – a razor was the one thing I didn't pack for this trip. My deck knife was definitely not the right option here – I'd tried – and my scissors died cutting the line from around the centerboard a month before, otherwise I would have tried those too.

My beard was rapidly being outdone though, by a large green and brown sea monster taking over the deck of the *ImpiFish*! Because my deck was constantly underwater, it had been colonized by a mass of very fast-growing, slimy, fur-like moss. This made my standing space even more slippery, like a sea slime carpet by day and even worse at night – pretty dangerous when conditions get tougher and wilder again. I had nothing to minimize it or eradicate its growth.

There was no manual for this, as there are no other little crafts out there like the *ImpiFish* that are as low in the water as mine, so my deck was submerged most of the time and hence becoming part of the sea. The ocean was trying to claim it for its own.

I tried to use the lid of the sunscreen as a scraper to scrub it off but that wasn't very effective. I would have to go back to wearing my Gul deck shoes by the end of the week, both to minimize the slipping and sliding across the deck from side to side and help the cuts I already had on my feet to heal. I had already damaged my big toe badly a couple days prior to this, when a rogue wave hit me and I slid while I paddled and braced myself across to the opposite side of the craft... bam! Damaged toe; little did I know at the time, I had actually broken it.

Earlier I'd been on deck doing my daily log, in light breeze conditions with a sea state not even a meter, when suddenly I sensed something and turned around just in time to see a rogue wave about to hit me. I ducked down and held the grab rail, in surf stance on the *ImpiFish* to try and catch it, but it hit fully side-on and I got completely drenched. Thank goodness I had my hatch closed, otherwise I would have been in serious trouble. It just goes to show, even though I know the ocean so well and had been out here over two months, I could still get caught off guard so easily. It can all go so very quickly wrong in a moment if you aren't careful and vigilant ALL of the time!

An hour later, I had just closed the back hatch after clipping on the autopilot when I was side-swiped by another pesky rascal 6-ft wave, square in the face. Thank goodness I was clipped on and braced for impact, but I just remember standing there soaked and laughing hysterically like a mad man, sea pirate/SUP guy.

It wasn't really funny at all, I was just depleted, but out here you have to learn to find the humor and the fun side of things, otherwise everything will overwhelm you and you'll just freak out, get negative and depressed and do something stupid or careless, so I just tried, each and every day, to roll with it and embrace every little magic moment and see them as a positive.

There would be big parts of this journey, especially being completely and utterly immersed in the moment out here, that I already knew I would miss deeply. I had the feeling that once I set foot on that dock, off the *ImpiFish*, life wouldn't ever be quite the same again.

Live in the moment, live in the now, take nothing for granted. Stop and enjoy the journey, before it's over and gone, as it can all change in a heartbeat, as we all know.

Appreciate all you have; your friends, family and loved ones around you, as that's all you have, all that matters, so make sure you know it, they know it, and they know you care.

# Things that go Bump in the Night

Atlantic Ocean | 18°39'16.54"N 57°37'17.40"W

I managed to get my autopilot working for the first time in a long time, so finally I could celebrate getting some proper restful sleep in my tiny cabin – or so I thought! But at 4:53 am, I was bumped awake by a chilling and strange noise, in the pitch black of the morning. Baaah! Grrrrrrr...

It was the most terrifying and intimidating sound. Something big was bumping and grinding down the side of the *ImpiFish*.

In an instant I knew exactly what that sound was... and it wasn't good!

There's no way to describe how terrifying that is in the middle of the night, when you are thousands of miles from any other human or land or help, and the creature that's outside your tiny little cabin is only separated from you by not even an inch of Nomex and fiberglass core, and the sound you are hearing is the sound of something very large, with teeth that could possibly sink you in a couple of bites if it decided to test you to see if you are a snack.

Think of a time in your early childhood when you were at home in the dark, alone. Maybe it was raining and windy outside and you're lying in your bed and suddenly you hear a really scary noise and you have no idea what it is. And you think to yourself, *Maybe if I just lie here and don't move and don't breathe it will go away.*

So there I was, still sort of holding my breath 20 seconds later, wondering if the sound I heard was what I thought it was and that's when it happened again. Baaah! Grrrrrrr...

The sound of something scraping down the side of my craft. I knew exactly what kind of creature it was. I'd seen one just a few days before.

And I knew it was testing the side of my craft to see what it would taste like.

Sharks have sensory receptors in their rough skin, so when they bump up against the side of you what they're actually trying to do is taste you. When they do that the first time that's a really bad sign. When they come around to do it a second time, that means that they liked what they tasted the first time and they're just coming back to do one last pass before they go up and take a big bite.

I think that's what was the most terrifying, knowing that a big shark like that shouldn't have come back and done a second pass; now I was just waiting to see if it was going to come back a third time. But I couldn't wait any longer. I realized I had shark repellent in a kind of shark grenade inside my little cabin, so I whipped it out, got into my safety gear, and jumped outside my cabin, holding on to the side in case it hit me again, either from the side or coming up from the deep below.

I put my hand into the water and pulled the pin on the shark grenade to disseminate the fluid into the water to deter the shark. At least, I hoped it would. It was supposed to scare away all sharks, and it had been tested on all sharks – except for Great Whites! And when I thought about this, I realized I was in the middle of the pitch-black night. I had my hand down in the water, releasing this fluid that hadn't been tested on Great Whites... and I couldn't see where the shark was. But I knew it was close.

So I took my hand out of the water, locked myself back in my tiny little cabin, and hoped and prayed that it wasn't going to come back again.

And luckily for me, it never came back. But for the rest of the next week, what I really couldn't get out of my mind was that it was the second time I had seen or heard a Great White, close to the craft, within a very short space of time. So that meant that either I was being tracked by the same Great White from before, or I was being followed by a different shark that also saw me as prey. And if that had happened with two different sharks in the same week, the likelihood was that there was going to be a third time, and maybe I wasn't going to be that lucky.

That was something that I really battled to process and get out of my brain.

They say what doesn't kill you makes you stronger. So maybe what doesn't scare you to death in the middle of the night makes you braver – or just grateful to be alive to see another day.

# Milestones and Mr Wings, the Flying Fish

## Atlantic Ocean | 18°31'29.26"N 58°8'25.26"W

On Friday February 10th, I hit my greatest milestone: the 44° W waypoint on my GPS. I now had only 1000 NM to go! Now that was worth celebrating.

Over the last two weeks of relentless wind and stormy seas, I noticed the *ImpiFish* listing to the one side (port side) again, which made me very nervous. I had a horrible feeling about this and I thought I might be taking in water again, since the little deck where I was standing, and where all my last crucial food and emergency water was stored, was constantly underwater.

It had been really distressing, seeing my feet and hatches underwater for the 10 days of heavy weather, wondering if they were flooding and not being able to check them, even though I was running out of food. I simply wasn't able to open and check the hatches unless conditions calmed down and went flat with a very light breeze – like now.

It was time for the moment of truth. *Holy shitballs!* The first hatch I checked had taken in almost 15 liters of water. It turned out there were also fewer food rations in my two main deck compartments than I had calculated, and worse, two of the daily ration packs had been ruined in the saltwater. *But I thought I had sealed it as tight as possible!* I was slightly panicked. I pulled everything out, pumped out all the water and replaced the hatch cover with the only extra new one I had.

I've said it once and yes, I will say it again: always have backup plans for absolutely everything!

I re-sealed and Vaselined the gaskets of every one of the hatches and then shut, secured and tightened all of them, as humanly and

Crabstick-tight as possible without actually damaging the thread of each hatch cover. I then pumped and sponged out the others, which, thank goodness, only had minimal water issues – less than three liters in each.

I realized I was now short on rations for the last 23 days. I was currently becalmed and only able to paddle 25 NM a day, which is half of what I should be doing to get me to Antigua in time.

I did some quick calculations and came up with two possible solutions to the new, very real issue at hand. I had planned for worst-case scenario and taken food for 95 days – 10 days more than I thought I would need. However, the Morocco to Canaries leg took almost 10 days longer than planned, with the storm and getting stuck on the sea anchor for two days before and after the islands, so there went the buffer extra 10 days rations. I'd had to discard five damaged ration bags due to weather/water damage, even though I recovered and salvaged part of two bags.

The good news was I still had some biltong (jerky) rations left, some Enduren Protein replacement drink, which I could use as extra meals, and my hydration mix.

The other thing I could make more of all the time, as long as I could charge my battery banks, was water, so this was super positive. Water is the only real essential, because as we all know hydration is everything. And I had enough coffee to get me through it all anyway. Coffee is also an amazing appetite suppressant, which under the current situation was great news! Even if not really ideal, as my body had been slowly eating itself and slowly breaking down for a while now. That's what happens on these long, extreme, solo endurance journeys.

Being slightly short on food was an awesome incentive for me to just paddle a little faster. And less food meant less cooking. Worst-case scenario, I was surrounded by an ocean of fresh fish, so, sushi – and I LOVE SUSHI!

*Don't worry Stripe, you're still safe. For now...*

And then a flying fish landed on my deck, which I aptly named: Mr

Wings! He gave me huge amounts of joy that morning, when I really needed a mental boost and a much needed ocean snack.

Mr. Wings was actually a really positive influence at a really difficult time. I was mentally badly affected by the two shark experiences I'd had in one week, and was battling to stay positive and unpack it mentally, knowing that I was a soft target for potentially more Great Whites.

So it really was awesome to come up onto deck and find this little creature there, even though he wasn't alive, after clearly getting his landing strip wrong. However he made me smile, as I was learning to celebrate the small things, anything to stay positive, and keep laughing through difficult and challenging times.

Mr Wings gave me so much happiness that day. I put his little wings out and made him fly around my craft for a while. I paddled with him for a couple of hours before I got hungry and ate him at lunchtime.

He was the tastiest treat I had had in weeks, after eating the same freeze-dried food packets for two months. As I was chomping Mr Wings, I made a pact with him. I wanted to say thanks because he gave me so much joy and reminded me to celebrate the small things and to keep a sense of humor through it all. So from that day onwards, every time I saw a flying fish I vowed I would shout 'Flying Fish!' and it would make me smile.

I kept my promise – I just never realized how many flying fish I was going to see from that point onwards! I literally saw hundreds. And I shouted every time. And every time I did that it made me smile – even though it became quite mundane. It made me realize that sometimes you have to fake it in order to become it… Do whatever you have to do to keep yourself smiling, positive and moving forward. And Mr Wings, the Flying Fish helped me do that.

# Don't Take a Break — Break Another Record!

Atlantic Ocean | 18°9'59.28"N 58°39'42.87"W

I'd been waiting till I got at least halfway across the Atlantic before trying to break the open ocean 24-hour, non-stop, unsupported world record for distance travelled over that time period. I wanted to wait till my craft was a little lighter, I was more comfortable and confident, and the conditions were right to do it properly.

On 17 February the conditions looked like they were going to be right – but this was the ocean, and as you will have learned by following this journey with me this far, unexpected stuff happens out here!

I started early at 6 am, and the first six hours were awesome. Then, out of the blue, I was suddenly becalmed. Then came wind from the south, completely opposite to the forecasted conditions.

My amazing forecaster – Leven-the-Legend – is right 90% of the time. But sometimes, local anomalies and conditions are hard to predict, especially out here. So be it! At least I got in some really good miles in that day while I was pushing as hard as I could to break the record.

I decided to wait for the trades to settle later in the week and try again. *If at first you don't succeed…*

After 72 days alone at sea I finally got all the conditions I was searching for to break the 24-hour record. Light 10–15 kn, with consistent slightly stronger gusts. I started at sunrise and pushed it all day, in super consistent trade-wind conditions, under beautiful sunny skies, with a following sea and breeze – it was as close to perfect as it gets. I maintained my hydration and recovery mixes, alternating them as I went, with consistent short breaks of 15–30 minutes, every 3 hours through the day and then every 2 hours through the night, until sunrise! By the time I clocked in at 6 am I had set a new 24-hour open ocean unsupported world record of over 50 NM.

The real challenge came after I finished and set the record. I had done such a great job managing myself and everything through the night, and had conditioned my body and mind so consistently over the last couple of months paddling 12–15 hours a day, that I actually felt really good, not broken at all, just super stoked, pumped and inspired.

I was super happy with the new record. I'd been searching for those perfect conditions for 72 days, and I knew once I found them I could crack the 60 NM mark.

I had planned to take a full 2–3 hour break, but I actually felt amazing after half an hour of food and hydration and 20 minutes relaxing in my little cabin. So amazing, in fact, that I just couldn't stop looking out at the conditions and going, *Holy smokes, it's still perfect out there…* So what was I doing lying here looking at it, if I could be out there capitalizing on these epic conditions to get the most miles possible, while it's possible? *Lying in this little cabin isn't going to get me across an ocean, so what are you doing Bertish? Get up and get out there!*

I asked Leven for an updated forecast on the conditions. The wind for the next 24 hours looked so good, with the sea state getting even smoother, and continued consistent light winds, that I just thought, *Screw it, why not try and break the record again? I've got nothing to lose and only miles to gain!*

I'd had almost an hour's break, from 6 am to 6:50 am. I felt great. The conditions were epic, so why not? What else am I going to do, sleep? Not when the conditions are so good. So I decided to copy and paste the magic recipe to the magic conditions.

In life, give it horns whenever the opportunity presents itself – you only have now and who knows what tomorrow may bring?

I had 10 minutes to send a message to the team to tell them I was resetting the clocks to start again at 7 am through to 7 am the next morning. *Here we go again, let's do this…*

This time the conditions were spot on all the way through the evening and the following morning: average wind speed 12–15 kn, with gusts in the 18 kn range. By the morning, I knew the *ImpiFish* and I had broken the previous day's record, but had we cracked the 60 NM barrier? I waited for Leven to do the numbers over the sat phone… Boom! We had covered 62,54 NM/115 km/71,97 km in 24/hrs. A new open ocean unsupported world record. Stoked!

I danced a little jig on my deck and laughed out loud, like a mad sea pirate. Then I went into my cabin and had my second last Bar One chocolate as my prize, to celebrate. I took an hour-and-a-half break and then went back out and got back to paddling!

Stack your monkeys, one after the next.

Just like that, I had achieved just under 150 NM in three days! Which is incredible in itself, but even better, it got me to under 700 miles from Antigua! And that's how you use mental distraction and focused goals to get you to an overwhelming target, while creating a way to get you to the finish quicker, so you don't run out of food.

I had been battling with the final distance mentally, but now I was practically there already, thanks to creating and chasing those golden monkeys!

And now I really was looking forward to taking a well-deserved break, before getting back out there and paddling again, until dark.

I still had almost 700 NM to go!

# Huckleberry Heroes

Atlantic Ocean | 18° 2'5.31"N 58°53'10.48"W

After the 24-hour records were completed, I paddled like a madman for five days, because the latest forecast told me the good weather was about to run out. There was a nasty low pressure on the horizon, a little depression affecting everything in my area and turning the breeze in the exact wrong direction.

I had to capitalize on the miles while I could, because things were getting pretty tight on my food rations. And as I came in for the final leg, I needed to get the approach angles right so I finished in Antigua and not Venezuela!

I received a message from someone on social media saying they were sailing to Antigua and should be passing me on the same course the following day. Would I mind if they came by to say hi and cheer me on?

I told them no problem, as long as the conditions were light and it was during the day. They gave me the yacht's name – *Huckleberry* – and I didn't think much more of it; I'd had a couple others mention they were going to pass by over previous weeks, but finding a small craft like mine is never as simple as it sounds in the middle of the Atlantic Ocean.

The next day dawned light and sunny, and just as I started my second shift I got a message from Ivan Wilken to say they were less than 40 NM away. *Awesome! This should be interesting.*

Two hours later, my AIS started flashing and 8 NM out off my aft quarter I see an incoming vessel. I grabbed my handheld VHF radio: '*Huckleberry, Huckleberry, Huckleberry*, this is *ImpiFish, ImpiFish, ImpiFish*, do you copy, over?'

Seconds later Ivan confirmed they'd picked me up on radar and were incoming. Within half an hour the SY *Huckleberry* came into view, a beautiful 44-metre ketch with seven crew waving and shouting from up on her bow. I hadn't seen another person for 72 days. The joy just bubbled up inside me.

I shot some footage and got a quick update on the weather and their expected ETA in Antigua. We shared some laughs mid-ocean, they asked me if I needed anything and I told them I had all I needed and they sailed away – but as they did they sounded their horn loudly and dropped something in the water behind them.

I paddled up to the little plastic bag, as I wanted to ensure that no plastic was left in the ocean and to my surprise, there was a note attached to the top of it: 'Keep up the good and inspiring work Chris. Enjoy the treats! From Ivan and the *Huckleberry* crew.' Inside was the most surprising gift ever: an ice-cold Coke, an orange, a chocolate and a 35 Euro donation towards the #SupCrossing charity initiative.

It might not have been a big thing for Ivan and the *Huckleberry* crew to stop by and say hi, but for a guy who hadn't seen land or another human being up close in a very long time, that encounter kept me smiling all day long.

I have to admit, it was the hardest thing, watching them sail off into the distance, when all I wanted to do was be onboard with them. I found myself following them as they disappeared into the distance, even though it wasn't the course I was meant to be taking… almost like a duckling following after its mother, not wanting to be left behind.

I had to laugh out loud, *This is ridiculous Bertish, get a grip bud, and get back on course.*

The definition of a hero is an ordinary person who finds the courage and strength to persevere and endure in spite of overwhelming obstacles.

I believe we all need heroes to admire, respect and look up to, and I've had many heroes in my life. My Dad, my Mom, some of my friends and numerous people I know that have battled through incredible adversity, tough times and illnesses, while still keeping their heads up and staying positive. All of them are my heroes. I never thought I'd have over two million people follow me on this epic journey, reading my 'Captain's Log' posts. I didn't think I would be getting personal inspiring messages from some of my greatest heroes and adventurers of our time – one came from super entrepreneur and adventurer Sir Richard Branson, another from the world's greatest modern-day adventurer, Sir Ranulph Fiennes. That day, it was also the *Huckleberry* crew.

The world needs more heroes, so go out and make a positive impact on the world; change a life; inspire a friend; be the best you can be. You will have a positive ripple effect on more people and lives than you will ever know!

I always say... Be a better human, each and every day in some small way.

# Personal Power Tools

Atlantic Ocean | 17°54'58.34"N 59°12'1.94"W

On Saturday 26 February I'd been 78 days alone at sea, and I had two weeks and 580 NM to go.

I'd taken over 1,5 million strokes. Every stroke bought a lunchbox and a smile, and I had about 350,000 ahead of me.

I had two split fingers and searing pain in my right shoulder and bicep, and I was running out of painkillers and anti-inflammatories, but the pain seemed temporary and I knew the positive impact of this project would last beyond my lifetime.

I was feeling driven, passionate and powered by a purpose stronger than money or records could ever give me.

I'd made great progress over the last 24 hours, getting in just under 50 NM as the wind swung back into the trades, ESE and ENE. But I wasn't done. I wanted to shift the paradigms of what was possible over the next 12 days, and average over 45 NM (83 km) each day until the finish.

That was the equivalent of a Molokai and a half every day, until it's done!

*I see it, I believe it, I will breathe it over the next 12 days and then I will achieve it.*

*Here we go Bertish, let's do this! Let's make it happen…*

Four days later, I had covered another 210 NM, averaging 52 NM per day, with 430 NM remaining to Antigua.

Actually getting to dry land felt about as far from reality as walking on the moon, but then I remembered what I'd accomplished already.

Two-and-a-half months ago, the possibility of having a ship come within two NM of me on AIS was terrifying. Just as impossible was the thought of the *ImpiFish* clocking up more than 5 kn on the speedometer, which I had almost doubled already, or being able to clock over 62 NM in 24 hours in such a heavy craft. But it's interesting, when you are constantly pushing your limits and your comfort zone, and when you start changing the way you look at things, the things you look at also begin to shift and change!

Over the last 80 days I had continually shifted my own comfort zones and personal paradigms, and watched the world's doubt change to support for what I was doing. Watching that all shift and the haters and naysayers come full circle was pretty powerful.

The words *Can't* and *Impossible* have always been firestarters for me. I used to call them 'dirty' swearwords, but I've come to realize that they have actually become my power tools. They are my motivators and catalysts for change – my two greatest tools for motivation, fuel to keep shifting my comfort zones, my paradigms, and transcending my limits in order to redefine the possible and set new parameters for myself and for others.

Within those two words lies your greatest self, greatest potential and opportunity and a new world you never even imagined, but it's lying dormant unless you believe and have the courage to try.

It all starts with the belief in self, and the realization that you can and you have the capability and capacity to do and achieve anything you want in life. If it's your purpose and you set your mind to it, you can do anything, including changing the world.

# The Squall Rider

Atlantic Ocean | 18°46'31.32"N 58°54'37.50"W

February became March and the miles behind me added up quick, while the ones in front of me dwindled. Antigua was now so close I could almost smell it. Almost…

Over the last week I'd been feeling a soft and guiding presence over my shoulder, in a positive sense. I can't really explain and all I can put it down to was having my Dad's presence with me, which I found really comforting. I'd started thinking about him a lot, and the following morning as I got up for my next shift I realized I'd had a strong and vivid dream of him speaking to me. He was telling me, crystal clear, that I needed to make sure my brothers were at the finish in Antigua. It was important, family is important; he would ensure it was all taken care of, I didn't need to worry about how. All I needed to do was call my brother, Conn on the satellite phone and tell him to tell my Mom that I'd had this message.

It was so real and powerful, that I turned on the satellite phone. It immediately got reception, which never happens. I dialed my brother's number and it instantly connected and went through, which had also never happened before.

Conn picked up and I delivered the message: call Mom and tell her the following. He phoned her right after our call. She responded without hesitating: she would pay for the tickets and they had to be there. Within a couple of days, both my brothers were on a plane heading to meet me in Antigua, exactly as the premonition had been delivered to me from my Dad, in the middle of the ocean! Now if that isn't powerful, I really don't know what is.

The last 10 days of the journey were possibly the most intense of my life. An Ironman marathon each day, without the luxury of changing disciplines to give some muscle sets a rest – or helpers along the way providing hydration and moral and medical support. And once I'd finished a session, I didn't get to sit back with a big cheeseburger and crack an ice-cold beer. In my break I would make dinner, re-work my navigation and routing, set up the autopilot, and sleep a couple of hours. Then I would wake up, re-check my mileage and distances and approach vectors, and paddle another 12–14 hours that day, that night and the next day, the next night, and the next, and the next – until I finished in Antigua, which I hoped would be late afternoon on Thursday 9 March, in a pumping 20–30 kn breeze!

It's hard to fight with someone who's not interested in arguing with you. When someone sends you hate or negativity, give back love and positivity. This relationship advice kept playing in my head over the next week, as I battled with a mean and unpredictable wind.

What were supposed to be light and steady 10–15 kn trade winds doubled abruptly to 20–30 kn trades and 3–4 m seas that had Captain Crabstick and *ImpiFish* hanging on for dear life, literally and figuratively.

I reached top speeds in super-intense conditions on 1 March, broaching badly in some big seas and getting flattened twice. On the last wild ride of the morning before it got too dangerous, the *ImpiFish* got hit in the stern from behind by a big breaking wave, and this pushed us into this giant, 4-m open-ocean peak, which I managed to surf down and stay in control, all the way to the bottom and buried the entire bow of the *ImpiFish* completely, while I was holding on to my paddle with one hand and the side of the *ImpiFish* with the other. As spray came right over the entire bow, the craft literally stopped, as the bow tried to resurface, then pulled hard to the left and broached, turning over sideways. I got flung over the one side, holding onto the main cabin top steel rail with one hand, trying not to go overboard. But as my hand and wrist buckled sideways, I knew if I didn't let go instantly

I would break my wrist, arm or both… so I released her and went overboard as the *ImpiFish* was moving at speed, which is super scary and dangerous! In my head I had done that split-second check before letting go: *Harness on and emergency tether clipped – check; big-wave leash on around my ankle and secure – check… Let go and grab for anything – let go now!*

In an instant I was in the water, under water, the ocean bubbles, wind, waves, chaos, BAM! The craft hit me on my head, then my back as she slowed down and tried to right herself, while I was being dragged along under the water and bashed up against the side of her. As she slowed I managed to pull myself back onboard by my harness, up and over the sidewall and rail, very shaken, scraped and bruised, just in time to see my water bottle and sunscreen floating away, with nothing I could do to get them back.

You never know how strong you can actually be, until you put yourself in a place where you have to muster all the courage you have within to get back up and keep on going and push through it.

*Okay, that was it!* This is when the extra set of squiddies were deployed over the stern and any other extra lines I could find to throw over the stern to slow her down. It wasn't even my intention to catch that big wave, it just happened. I realized in that one moment how dangerous that was; and I had broken my one communications aerial and I couldn't let that happen again, ever, in these bigger seas. So no more of that, that was the last surfing ever in the big stuff. Wind chop is fine, but the open ocean swells… too dangerous.

*That will never happen again,* I said to myself, as I nursed my scrapes with mercurochrome ointment, checked the lump on my head and tested my wrist.

Moving on and moving forward. Note to self: be the tortoise, not the hare, and you will still win the race. This race is about finishing and finishing in one piece, not about speed. It's that simple.

A couple of days later I knew the breeze was going to build and there might be some pretty volatile moments. Squalls are pretty scary mid-ocean, because they come at you at pace with huge cumulonimbus clouds, black and ominous, with a raging sea underneath them. They bring winds of 25–45 kn and blinding rain, but they are normally quick and intense, over within 20 minutes to half an hour.

In the beginning of this adventure, I would duck into my cabin when squalls approached and wait them out. But as I got more comfortable with everything deeper into my journey, and because I needed to get in those miles and save rations by getting there faster, I started analyzing my attitude. Could I shift my mindset, change my perception to create different way of looking at them, in order to get more positive results?

I started to focus on trying to see squalls, in a new way, as opportunities in disguise. They became my secret little mile-enhancing weapons, to help me get extra distance and speed. I would just have to learn to harness the fear, tap into it as fuel, learn to love them and ride them out!

The only way to not fear the storm is to shift the way you see it: embrace it and become the storm!

I'd been through pretty much everything, so I thought, *Why not let's give it a try?* So I shifted out of my comfort zone and when I saw a squall coming, I started laughing. *Hell yeah, bring it on, let's get ready, let's go!*

I clipped on my harness, big wave leash on, all my squiddies deployed, locked and loaded, and got ready to ride the white lightning! My mental challenge was to see what top speed I could get through the squall without broaching – and maybe get some surf time in too!

Go the *ImpiFish* – I cracked 7,4 kn, then 9,2 kn, which is over 15 km/h. That was full-blown surfing speed, mid-ocean, on a craft that shouldn't really be out there at all. Stoked!

# The Final Storm

I'd been alone at sea for 90 days now and had 162 NM to go.

Navigating without sails or an engine requires everything you got, skill, courage, heart, focus, grit, constant vigilance and then some. As we came closer to Antigua, I focused even more intently on the approach angles, routing and weather, because if I got it wrong, I would possibly miss the entire Caribbean island chain.

I had to paddle as many miles as possible each day, but I also had to get north; the wind was predicted to change to go NE for the last two-and-a-half days, so once I reached my waypoint, I'd need to change my course from dead downwind, before I could come off the autopilot and go onto my crab-drogue sideways system, altering my course by almost 40 degrees to crab-tack my way north until the morning.

When I did this I lost miles and my speed dropped by half, but if I didn't do it I wouldn't get far enough north, and wouldn't make the angle for the waypoint to reach Antigua, and would end up somewhere near Guadeloupe or Barbados. (Even though Barbados is one of my favorite islands, it wasn't where I needed to go right now – and I didn't have a visa or another two weeks' worth of food with me, which is how long that could take!)

I had learned to flow with nature and what the ocean had in store for me. I knew it would all work out just the way it was meant to, so I just had to get up each day, do the best I could, give it all I had, let go of the rest and just trust in the process.

I'd done my inventory and had just enough supplies – and most importantly, coffee – for another week, so I could hold out until the 9th or 10th March. I was going to need the caffeine – the conditions over the next four days were going to be super-intense. The wind was predicted between 20–30 kn NE/ENE, but I would only really know the wind angle the next afternoon when it filled in. When that happened I would be very limited in regards to my routing – but once I'd passed the eastern tip of any of the islands, be it Antigua or Guadeloupe, the full crossing would be complete and my team could help guide me in.

*We'll make it work, no matter what…*

Famous last words.

When the tail end of a bad low-pressure system heading north hit me, I was forced to be on sea anchor unexpectedly for 30 hours. Being stuck in my cabin, watching myself going back toward Africa at one mile an hour on my tracker, when I was already short on rations and not being able to do much about it, was probably one of the most difficult things to endure. But I had no choice; it's just not possible to paddle into 30 kn of headwind – never mind what it does to the sea state.

But by the next morning, after almost 30 hours inside my cabin painstakingly watching my hard-earned miles disappear from the day before, I couldn't take it any longer. I got to the point where I was like, *Okay enough, that's it, I'm not going backwards any further, that's it, I'm done, I don't care what direction I go, but I'm not going backwards even one more mile.*

I decided I needed to get out there and paddle, even if it was in the wrong direction!

The wind eased slightly to about 15–20 kn and was due to get lighter that afternoon, so I pulled up the sea anchor and got moving. I didn't even care what direction I was going, or if I was just battling into or across the wind and not moving forward at all, as long as I wasn't going backwards, that simple! At that point any decision and action felt better than none. I knew it was going to be super tough, but I couldn't expect different results unless I got up and changed what I was doing; I needed to take action and be the change I wanted to see, in order to get the result I intended to create.

When I did my forecast update with Leven that night, he was super happy that I had already started paddling north, which he hadn't expected, but told me that I needed to paddle north even further, because another storm was going to come in directly after the front I was currently in, over the next three days. And if I didn't get to a certain waypoint within those four days, then I was going to get pushed so far south when the wind turned, that I was going to miss the Caribbean island chain completely and end up in Venezuela. I definitely didn't have a visa for that, and definitely not enough food, so there was no way that I was going to miss it, no matter what it would take!

So I had to step everything up and paddle across the conditions for another three-and-a-half days. That meant paddling on one side, not even able to change my stroke onto the other side. I would literally have to be paddling on the left hand side (port side) for four days, 12 to 15 hours a day, which would pull on my bicep even more. (I didn't know it at the time but I had damaged my rotator cuff so badly at this point it was starting to pull my bicep off my shoulder blade!)

I had just run out of painkiller tablets too. But I just had to focus on getting to that waypoint, no matter what, because I knew I couldn't miss it.

I tried to figure out from all that I'd learned on the journey, what the storm was likely to do and if I got to that key waypoint, what the direction of the wind was going to be in order to be in the right place to come into Antigua with the wind behind me – crucial, even though the chances of me actually getting that right in these conditions was like finding a needle in a haystack...

When I had to finally get some rest, I put out the parachute anchor, then locked off my steering system to the side, so I was zig-zagging across and down the course. That meant even when I wasn't on shift, or was sleeping, I wasn't getting pushed totally in the wrong direction.

On that last and final morning, after three hours sleep, the wind was predicted to change as the storm swung south. At 3:30 am, I got up one last time and turned the craft onto the course to have Antigua directly on my bow, right ahead… and felt the wind perfectly on my back. Meaning the wind was almost directly behind me, the perfect angle and the perfect course as I turned towards Antigua. The chances of me pulling that off… were one in a million.

To be able to get that right, to get the navigation so spot on, with the limited range of steerage and angles I could travel on my little craft was like a miracle really… To get to that exact point and for the wind to be able to turn to that direction where it was perfectly on my back, felt almost like destiny!

It was like the universe said: *Okay, you've done everything we've asked of you. You've gone through all we have dished out and you have made it work and we can't give you any more. So we're going to give you this one gift on your final day, and that is to have the wind and the conditions at your back for the last 20 NM. We're giving you everything you need to be able to get you there for this final test.*

The wind and the weather and the sea state were still crazy intense and scary, but at least it was all coming from behind me, which made it almost manageable. If the wind had been 30 to 50 degrees off in any other direction, I would have been screwed.

It was the greatest reward and gift from the universe to let me fulfill what I had set out to achieve. And if it wasn't for that one small blessing, there's no way I would have made it. It took everything, all the knowledge and experience to be able to make that call, and get to that point, and then get it right.

And that's when I first saw the lights of Antigua directly ahead of me in the distance.

# Bringing it all Home

Atlantic Ocean | 17°21'47.37"N 61°9'58.10"W

When dawn broke a couple hours later, on 9 March I had already been paddling for an hour. I knew this would be my last sunrise out here after 93 days alone at sea.

When I first caught sight of the lights of Antigua in the far distance it was 4 am and still pitch black outside. I was in full weather gear because the storm was so wild, and I had my VHF radio hooked onto my harness, ready to contact the harbor – I knew the guys were going to try and come out to meet me when I got close, to help guide me in, if they could, but the weather was so wild, I didn't know if any boat could or would be able to get out in this. It all felt surreal.

When the sun peeked its way through the clouds early that morning, an incredible gold light beamed down ahead of me, among the dramatic black and stormy sky. It was so beautiful. It was as if it was beckoning me on. Me, this little speck on my ImpiFish in the middle of the vast Atlantic Ocean.

If my navigation had been just 10 degrees off in either direction, I would have missed the island completely.

The more than 2 million strokes since I'd left Morocco had wreaked havoc on my body and my shoulder, but at that moment I felt no pain.

The 10 NM to the finish would take me about three hours. I knew my brothers and friends were waiting to meet me, as well as Leven, the one person who had been my lifeline through this entire epic journey.

I had visualized this moment so vividly over the past five years, but what I had envisaged and what I got were very different, mainly because the weather was just so intense. And it wasn't over yet.

I had GPS coordinates for where I needed to come into, but it was intense coming in with these huge seas and heavy weather. The seas were so crazy, in fact, that the coastguard, who was supposed to bring Leven out to guide me in, decided the conditions were too hectic!

Instead I saw this long, thin boat trying to punch out through these giant seas – turns out a cigar boat was the only boat that could get out in those conditions, that's how wild it was out there. Then I saw my brothers Greg and Conn, and my buddy Jeff Clark and Brian Overfelt on the deck. They were being skippered out through the storm by an Antiguan legend, and America's Cup sailor, Shannon Falcone.

It was wild and windy and stormy and intense. As they came punching out through the maelstrom, I think the conditions really brought home for everyone on that boat just what I'd been dealing with 24/7 for the last 93 days. It was almost too big for them to comprehend that this was what I'd been doing alone for the past three months.

It was a pretty incredible moment to see them coming out through that massive heaving sea, at first light that morning. It will be etched into my heart and mind forever. But I was still in full combat mode, laser focused, just trying to navigate my way in towards the lee of the island; I had to be so precise and not make a mistake in the finish. I knew I would probably lose it and get emotional afterwards, but at that point I was just stoked to see them coming out and super focused to get to the finish.

I think it was far more emotional for everyone on the boat, finding me as this little green light coming through that stormy chaos, with massive waves and howling winds, coupled with the dark, ominous dawn sky. I think it was overwhelming for them to see their brother out in these radical conditions alone and understand what I had been doing alone for over three months.

Later, both my brothers put it into their own words. Greg sent a WhatsApp to our good friend Spike, from Wavescape:

*You do not understand how hardcore this guy is and what*
*I witnessed today. Truly the most remarkable feat by any*

*adventurer of our time. I saw a guy who tamed an ocean, who rode a self-designed craft and became one with it in some of the most crazy ocean conditions I have witnessed – 15 miles off Antigua riding wild scary mountains. This was into the beyond!!!!! And this was only a small taste of the life-threatening voyage alone for 93 days! Truly inspirational.*

And this from my brother Conn:

*It's still hard to comprehend what @Chrisbertish was doing when we saw him coming out of the darkness miles off the coast of Antigua. Yes we were stoked to see him, beyond stoked, but what struck us was the disbelief in what we were actually seeing. As a trio of brothers we've surfed big waves, sailed storms and stand-up paddled crazy winds together, but what we witnessed Chris doing at 5:32 am in the morning through a heaving 10 ft open ocean swell was nothing short of creative artistry – and one of the most beautiful things I have ever seen.*

*It was magic and surreal – a fantastic blend of awe-struck doused with confusion; the kind humans get when there's no reference for what they are seeing, an encounter that forces one to reconsider the reality you've become accustomed to. This was a WTF moment of magnificent proportions. Because Chris wasn't just paddling across the ocean, he was literally riding it – entirely at one with the craft, the swell, the wind and the entire ocean landscape. He was part of it – not a human on it – he was it.*

*And that flow, in my view, is the highest form of human art that exists.*

*Mozart, Picasso, Da Vinci; take a bow to a fellow master: My bro Chris Bertish.*

It was an honor to have grown up with these amazing brothers, both legends, great humans and watermen themselves. But while they were having their WTF moment, I just wanted to get to where it was quiet enough that I could trigger my flare and signal the end of this epic journey.

Usually a boat that comes in solo in challenging conditions like these without an engine, will be met by a towboat, which will connect up a tow line and pull it in for the last few miles into Nelson's Dockyard. But I wanted to see if my navigation was good enough to paddle in.

English Harbour is surrounded by massive cliffs, called the 'Pillars of Hercules'. There were waves smashing up against the cliffs and I had to come super close to them, to stay protected from the wind, which was blowing across me, as I came into the harbor. Everything else around me disappeared; I literally only saw what was right in front of me, I was so focused on making sure I didn't make a mistake getting in. The last thing I wanted after traveling across an entire ocean was to make a mistake at the end – I could see the headline: '*Man almost paddles across Atlantic Ocean and then gets shipwrecked on the side of the Caribbean Island!*'

I had to be completely focused on getting in to the lee of the island to get some shelter from the wind. But that was easier said than done. I couldn't have thought of a better place to finish this journey, which was such a Herculean one! No one had ever done this before – basically navigated from one continent to an island 20 km in size, which is like a pinprick on the other side of the Atlantic, with no functional steering system, navigating without sails or an engine in these wild conditions...

As I got closer to English Harbour the excitement rose inside me. I cranked up the sound system to blast 'Impi', by Johnny Clegg and Jaluka, in honor of my homeland, and the brave little craft that had carried me safely across an entire ocean.

When I finally got in to the lee of the island, to a quieter and more protected space, I triggered the flare. As I raised my arm to signal the end of this incredible journey, I bellowed a mighty, primal victory roar and let out everything that had been pent-up inside me for the last three months. It was done, the weight lifted off my shoulders and the immense burden and duty and responsibility I had taken on and felt for so long, had finally been fulfilled. I was finally free.

# English Harbour

Antigua | 17°0'58.92"N 61°42'21.53"W

I was sorely disappointed not to see Leven on the boat that came out in those giant seas with my brothers – he was the person I had trusted more than any other to get me through the last four months, but ironically, he had been stuck on shore with the coastguard! So it was great to finally see him when he came out to greet me in a tiny little boat just as I was coming around into the harbor entrance. More than any other person, he knew what it had taken for me to cross more than 7500 km of hazardous open ocean, alone, paddling for 93 days straight.

As we came into the harbor we were flanked by more than 20 super yachts, all between 100 and 300 ft long, lined up like a welcoming committee. I paddled up this channel of yachts all blowing their horns, their crews up on deck in uniform, shouting and clapping. It was like being in a massive amphitheater – I felt like a gladiator, arriving victorious in the Colosseum.

It seemed that the entire port and town had come down to celebrate my journey. Then the clouds parted and the sun shone down rays of light – everything opened up in this beautiful magic blue moment. I finally got to the dock, completely under my own power, with the use of that one, small single blade paddle, and as the welcoming party of over fifty people standing on the dock pulled me in and secured the *ImpiFish* finally to the side of the dock, I just let go and fell back into the water.

What happened after that was all a bit of a blur. Clells was there. She came and gave me a big hug and kiss and wrapped me in a huge South African flag. I gave a very passionate and emotional impromptu speech, and then I was given a beer and a hamburger. I was waving it around while I was speaking and signing books and t-shirts and then I don't really know what happened after that. There was champagne being sprayed, beers and people asking loads of questions. There was meant to be a full physical check-up with the medics – but they took one look at me speaking on the dock to the crowd and waving my hamburger around and just pronounced me healthy – well, except for having lost 20% of my body mass.

Besides Nancy Ward, David Becker and Leven that were there from my team, there were about 15 friends and family who flew in from all over, and then there were other people who had flown in from around the world, just because they'd been following the journey and found it so inspiring. Hundreds of thousands more followed my arrival on Facebook Live coming in at the finish. That was just incredible to me, to realize that my journey had had that kind of impact.

The celebration of the ending of this incredible journey, but the beginning of yet another roller-coaster next chapter…

# Epilogue

Flying home over the Atlantic Ocean, I remember looking down on that vast expanse that I had just stand-up paddled over and thinking to myself, *It's not possible!* I had to catch myself and say, *Well, you've just done it – you just paddled across the entire Atlantic Ocean on a stand-up paddleboard.* It just didn't seem real. But it was. I had done it – because I never stopped believing that I could.

I hope that you've enjoyed this book, that it inspires you and might have a positive impact or change your life, even if it just gives you the little extra faith and belief in yourself that you need to try something new, or to do that one something you have always dreamed of doing.

That's why I do what I do, and will continue to do, because I know it helps and inspires so many, being the catalyst for some positive change in others, reminding us all what we are capable of and what's possible when we dig deep and have the courage to try. And if you can raise some money to help disadvantaged kids or pay for life-changing operations at the same time, even better.

Ordinary people accomplish extraordinary feats, inspire and change the world, every single day, all through the power of self-belief and a powerful purpose. You can do and be anything you want in life. It's just a choice – and then, having the courage to follow your heart, take daily steps and actions in the direction of your goals and dreams.

When you have a mission and a vision that you're not prepared to let go of no matter what, ignore what other people say or think. Just break it down into little bite-sized chunks and focus on what's in front of you, take it day by day, stroke by stroke, mile by mile… When you continue doing that consistently and you never, ever give up, you will eventually get to the end goal and achieve it – as long as you don't stop trying.

You really can do anything you want in life – even things that you may think are impossible!

When you are ready, you will get exactly what you need. It's the law of the universe and the power of the source!

You just have to be ALL IN and then take action to make it happen. It really is that simple!

### The Charity and Give-back Aspects of the SUP Crossing

The Atlantic SUP Crossing raised just under R1 million for charitable causes. The funds were used to pay for one hundred cleft palate operations, through Operation Smile, and more than a thousand meals were donated through The Lunchbox Fund to disadvantaged children.

Offering lunch helps to get learners to school to receive an education. In addition, my team and I donated money to the Signature of Hope Trust, which empowers young minds through literacy programs. We also collaborate with Maryke Musson of the Two Oceans Aquarium, assisting with educational videos that aim to raise awareness of the importance of the ocean.

# What Next? Pacific Ho!
## (Or, Birds on the Wing and the Art of Flight)

I finished my transatlantic crossing in March 2017. By the end of the year I was already planning my next adventure – I had found my new passion.

While crossing the Atlantic Ocean, often I would just stop paddling and be in pure awe of the open ocean birds on the wing, mostly the stormy petrels and the beautiful, big and graceful albatrosses gliding and surfing the big ocean swells, some even while they were sleeping, using the tips of their wings as sensors to gauge their distance from the water. It was pure poetry in motion. Sometimes I would stand there for 10 or 20 minutes and just admire the beauty, harmony and perfect definition of FLOW they represented. They had become one with the elements and their natural surroundings.

After 70 days out at sea alone on my tiny little *ImpiFish*, I got into a very similar space. I find it hard to explain to most humans back on land, but that incredible gliding, surfing the air sensation I witnessed and was so in awe of…

I found exactly that in the hydrofoil.

There are very few sensations that even come close to wrapping a long, drawn-out 200-degree arc, at speed, tapping into the pure, raw energy of the source. There really is nothing like gliding silently *above* the water on a hydrofoil.

It took me a while to get to this point. It was a frustrating learning curve and one of the hardest things I have ever done. It has also been incredibly humbling. It's good for all of us to go back to learning something new from scratch, but like with everything in my world, I see the greatest potential in everything – and with this new sport, the future looks incredible.

*When you shift your mindset, attitude and are prepared to challenge yourself, evolve and embrace change, everything you see around you changes too!*

Foiling as a sport is difficult to explain, but as soon as you find yourself gliding above the water, in effortless silence, like an albatross flying above the ocean waves, everything makes sense and you realize it's like no other feeling on the planet! It's pure focus, freedom and joy personified.

When you break it down, foiling is simply the most efficient use of the wind and ocean energy that exists on the planet. So much so that all sports in the water that *aren't* on foils seem somehow slow and inefficient by comparison!

I've only been foiling for four years and it's completely transformed my life. I started learning to foil waves in the same way as surfing, just smoother and with more flow than on a surfboard. Then I started towing into massive waves like Dungeons and Tafelberg (it's truly scary how hard you hit the water when you fall from a foil), to connecting waves all over South Africa and then Hawaii, miles offshore doing down-winders…

For the first time in 25 years, I was stoked again surfing in 2-foot surf – as foiling makes even small, poor quality waves feel like clean, 4–6 foot waves, because foiling is so efficient. Which means you are stoked all the time!

Then came the progression to kite foiling and then winging (wing-surfing) and my mind was officially blown. Being able to tap into the raw source energy of the bumps miles offshore, and ride them, literally for hours…

I took a trip to Hood River in Oregon to improve my winging skills, joining an awesome crew in 30–40 kn of wind, doing a down winder riding 5–8 foot wind chop 13 miles up a river for 2 hours. Surfing waves on a foil with the wing merely there helping me connect to the next big lump to the left or right of me…

It was around this time that I was talking to some friends around a fire, in Mexico, after a foiling session. One of them said, 'Imagine if you could wing foil across an ocean?'

Someone piped up, of course, with my favorite line... 'That's impossible!'

'Is it?' I asked with a smile.

∎ ∎ ∎

*Three months before this book went to print, **Chris had just completed the first ever solo, unsupported "Wing-foil" journey across the Pacific – 2450NM from California to Hawaii, 48,5 days, completed on July 19th 2022.***

*Watch this space, and wait for the next book, coming in 2025! (In the meantime, you can find Last Known Coordinates, his film about the Transatlantic SUP Crossing, on Google Play Movies, YouTube, and Apple iTunes.)*

# Acknowledgments

A very special thanks to these amazing people that all contributed to my life and this journey in some small, or some massive, way.

- Fran Bertish – thanks for being the solid Mom, the rock you are for us all. I'm sorry to always make you worry and for choosing a very different path that has taken me around the world and away from the conventional norm. I love you very much and couldn't wish for a better mom in the world, thanks for always being there for me, no matter what! (And for being the hero who got both brothers to meet me at the finish in Antigua!)
- Keith Bertish for being the legend and hero he always was to me and still is.
- Andrew Hoeks – thanks for the love and friendship always, it's been an incredible journey; you're an incredible friend and legend. Looking forward to the next chapters together my friend.
- Pauli and Lulu Copson – thank you to my special friend Paul and super Lulu – so many good times and memories together, too many to mention, but never forgotten, and so many more good times to come. I got your back always my friend, always and forever.
- Rebecca Cully – thanks Super Turtle for the love and support, for all the special chapters we've already shared on this journey together. The great times, laughs, sunsets and memories. So much love for you and the journey we've shared together.
- Pam Fitzsimons – thanks for all the love and support on my journey, over the last couple years, with the family.
- Conn Bertish for being the brother you have always been, with many more positive times to come in the future.
- Greg Bertish for being Greg. Hopefully in the future we can one day get back to the place we once were.
- Leven Brown – for everything you did for me on this journey and the next one. You are one in a million Captain and I couldn't have done either of these big expeditions without you. You legend!
- Sir Richard Branson for your support, inspiration and for having me come and visit Necker island and talk with you and your team. I know my paddle has a good home at Necker with you. Looking forward to working with you and the team again in the future.

- Alan van Gysen – thanks for all the help and support in Agadir, and the great pics as always.
- Ace (Adrian Charles) – thanks for the help in Agadir, brother.
- Jason Rade – for all the help with everything you do all the time my friend.
- Mandy Scanlen – thanks for coordinating some of the Crossing partners.
- Kirsti Lyall – for the PR help in SA for the project.
- Kelly Burke (Flux Communications) – thanks for all the help with my PR and coordination of media stuff over the years, you're a superstar.
- Ashleigh Acker (Ace Agency) – thanks for all the help with my PR in the USA and coordination of media stuff over the years, you're a star.
- Bruce McDonald – thanks for all the help with everything, always, from the films to family, to life… But mostly just for being the special, loving and caring human you are, the love and friendship, from you and your family, always.
- Maryke Musson – thanks for the awesome friendship, turtle rescuing, shark freediving, fun times and amazingness all around… you rock Roctopuss, my favorite fish lady, and thanks for the amazing mermaid cards on my journey to keep me sane.
- Jeff Clark – thanks for always being there for me through thick and thin over the years.
- Shannon Falcone – thanks for all the help and support through the finish of the Crossing and beyond. You such a champion and a legend.
- Brian Overfelt – thanks for all the photos, Mavs days, OPL nights and support along my journey.
- David Becker – thanks for all the help with everything, the mental stuff, training and audio packages, but mostly just for being the special and genuine human you are, the love and friendship, from you and your family, always. Love you brother.
- Doug Boyes – a friendship that stands the test of time, always there for you if and when you need me brother.
- Craig Featherby (Carrick Wealth) – thanks for the support for the Crossing journey.
- Arthur (Island Tribe) – thanks for all the support on the journey always, you champion.
- Barry Pauw (Enduren) – for the awesome product and support always bud.
- Racefood (Wedgewood) – thank you for the awesome product.

- Clellind Fivaz – thanks for all the good times, memories, the journey through this time of the book, the love and friendship always, you're such a special and amazing human.
- Darren Robertson – good times and challenging times, we've been through it all and will continue to do so until the end. Proud of you brother.
- Loren Robertson – thanks for the support of Darren through it all...
- Jacqui L'Ange, my editor – thanks for all you do and the great friend you have become over the years. Couldn't have put these books together without you and I always enjoy my time up in the woods with you, Stokey the rooster, the doggies and horses.
- Lewis Pugh – my inspiration, a champion, legend and good friend.
- Ingeborg Pelser, my book manager – thanks for all the help on this journey to the second book and hopefully many more.
- Nicholas Maunder – thanks for the help on the Crossing project and all the good old sailing times. Part of the foundation that allowed me to complete this one and survive and stay alive.
- Lynelle Ranft – thanks Linnie always for the friendship over the years and all the help with all the medical stuff with the project...
- Jane Hoskins – to a very special friend I've known for more than 22 years now and many more special rainbows, chats and memories to create in the years still to come.
- Garth Rossiter – thanks for the love and friendship always my friend. To the Three Ships and beyond.
- Grant and Kells Jenkinson – thanks for the love and friendship always.
- Mustafa – thanks for all the help in Agadir getting the visa stuff sorted when it expired.
- Val Doar – thanks for always being there through the years. Once your cabin boy always your cabin boy!
- Annie McPhillips – sweetie pie, legend and champion of the Caribbean and just super cool chick and friend.
- Mike Firmin – thanks for all the good sailing times over the last decade or more and always supporting me through the years. You're a great human and great friend. I really appreciate you.
- Alberto Possati – thanks for the good times, speed sailing, windsurf times, the guitar lessons, mentorship, amazing friendship, help and always supporting me through thick and thin over the last 6 years. *Grazie mile.*

- Professor Timothy and Marilyn Noakes – thanks for being the legend you are and all the great advice, feedback, help, love, friendship and support over the years. Hopefully a couple more surfs in together before the end of the year.
- Nancy Ward – a friend, helper, ambassador and great person all around. Thanks for being such a big help for the SUP Crossing project and beyond.
- The Melk family – Filpert and Henriette, thank you for your support. Always in my thoughts… RIP my special friends.
- Steve Pike for the awesome tracking, friendship and posts along my journey and through the Big 4 Big Wave mission in the early 2000s.
- Craig Middleton – thanks for the sailing mentorship, since I was 15 years old, over the years, the advice on routing and weather and just for being the legends you are Craig and Carol.
- Ben Grenata – thanks for being my team and backup in the UK over the years, miss you brother, you such a champion and a legend. Never change, but always wrestle that Annacoda, always.
- Doogle – thanks for the good times, the bad times and the wave sliding and laughs in-between brother.
- Craig Kolesky – thanks for all the epic pics, great shoots, adventures and all that's still to come… Thanks for supporting my journey always. You, my friend, are a gentleman and a legend.
- Steve Hurt – thanks for being the friend you are and the friend you have become, so grateful to have such meaningful friends in my life I've known for over 20 years.
- Greg Casey – for the friendship and mad times, the 'bowl of milk' and all the surf beer travel times, the Mentawais and Mexico and many more to come. You are the inspiration and ambassador for the good times and living life to the full – a balanced life.
- Ant Kyle – for the good old times and current times and times to come, stay the legend you are.
- Rob Baigrie – Baigrie, you champion… you are a good man and even tho it's been a short journey, it's also been a long one in the making. I value you and our friendship and hope through this next journey I can make you proud and give Arena more cool stories she can follow and share with her class.
- Anthony – 'El Presidente' – Champion and legend. Always stoked and proud to have you part of all my journeys and adventures, both the ocean ones and the land-based building ones… looking forward to the next chapter together brother. *Grazie.*

- Johnny van der Vyver (Mr Friday Island) – thanks for all the help, guidance, friendship and support over the years. Aloha!
- Tess and Rishu Strzelecki – thanks for all the sailing days a decade ago and for all the fun times at the farm, St Francis, our plot, our friendship and shared Mona the cat!
- Linzi Hawkin – a long time, we've had some ups and downs but you'll always be important to me and know I'm always there for you.
- Ard Matthews and Ross Learmonth –thanks for the amazing music that helpedme cross the Atlantic and your friendship and good times thereafter.
- Cassandra Rose - Thanks Cass for all the love, friendship and support always - you Superstar you!
- Peter Peterson - Thanks Pete for always helping on my SUP journeys from near the beginning. Paddling and supporting me and always by my side, leading right up to my Atlantic crossing.
- Rob Munro -Thanks for my first boards and the one I Sup'd Dungeons on, which was definitely not designed for that at all. Thanks Rob, the Champ you are.
- Steve & Terri Lee- Thanks for all the help and support over the years, love you guys.
- A big shout out to the Southern Glazer Wines and Spirits team for their support.
- Thanks JP, Nic, Lisa and the HotInk Team for all the help and support always.

Thanks to all the photographers who have helped by contributing to this amazing story with their epic images. I'm so grateful and appreciative of your help and support along my journey. Thank you.

## Crowdfunding Supporters

Thank you to all below that supported me on the crowdfunding campaign in 2020, for this book and the journey to getting it finished. You are all legends: Karen Marvin, Brian McLaughlin, Simon Henley, James Mellor, Chris Grippo, Ayelet Baron, Dave Fulwood, Wanda Bowles, Alberto Possati, Adrian Hougham, Robert Baigrie, Jane Hoskins, Rebecca Cully.

I'm sorry to anyone I've met over the years where I haven't given you the time you were hoping, or who caught me on a bad day when I was rushing and wasn't as friendly as I could have been... we all have our bad days/moments and are dealing with different things at different times on our own journeys. I'm still human and far from perfect and don't always show up at my best, even though I always try! Like everything in life, it's a constant work in progress and each and every day, in some small way, I'm trying to be a better version of myself, even hough I don't get it right all the time.

Thanks all for the patience and understanding – the ups and downs make us, shape us, but don't define us! Strive each and every day to just be a little better than you were the day before. Stay stoked and keep going ALL IN for what you believe in... each day is not a given, it's a gift, that's why it's called the present, so don't take it for granted. Go out and have an adventure, as you never know what's possible until you try.

No regrets, only great experiences, moments and memories.

# Speaking Engagement Shouts / Testimonials

*Chris is an amazing human!! Hearing how he maintained his positivity and mental health through his incredible voyage is amazingly inspirational. His talk was very timely; reminding us of the essential elements and tools required to maintain a positive outlook during these trying times. Chris's authentic delivery and positive energy left our team uplifted and inspired!"*
KATRINA TEMPERO - UX Manager, Google

*He's an expert on shifting his comfort zone, and it's clear through his public speaking that he is right in his comfort zone. He teaches on finding your greatest potential, and coming from such a legend as Chris, I was left feeling empowered to evaluate where in my life I could more intentionally "dial it up" and follow my passions. If there's ever an attitude for gratitude that should be shared on a big stage (or virtual event), then Chris' story is one for the records. This was one of our most successful talks at Salesforce."*
KELLY COWDEN – Events Manager, Salesforce

*His incredibly inspiring talk stuck deeply in my mind and motivated me to: get back into fitness, take on intentional nutrition for health rather than just pleasure, re-engage in the practices that put my feet and mind back on the ground so I can be present and in the moment by moment excellence of our human experience (My wife and family thank him). I take my hat off to Chris and thank him for the gift of his boggling and articulate story of how far beyond the place where we usually stop in life, we really can go."*
MICHAEL EASTWOOD - Senior System Engineer, Jet Propulsion Laboratory, NASA

*After an inspiring address based on his beautiful and courageous true story, Chris deservedly received a massive standing ovation from our international audience in financial services. His story is simply Breathtaking! "*
MIKE LEE - CEO, ATMIA Global

*Chris provided us with an authentic view of his own isolation experiences and shared top tips that were easy to incorporate into daily life to help us navigate through this crisis and even beyond. I believe anyone could benefit from learning and applying these tools in their life. Extremely grateful to have been a part of this session and to have shared in the wisdom of Chris's insights."*
VANESSA GILL - Regional Manager, Cisco ANZ

*Chris was an amazing part of our event and brought his incredible journey and mission to life on the PagerDuty Summit stage. The audience was captivated by his storytelling and humor. We are incredibly grateful for the inspirational example he sets for us all! Everyone left highly inspired and energized!*
JENNIFER TEJADA - CEO, Pager Duty

If you want to book Chris as a speaker, contact him through *www.chrisbertish.com*

## Social Media

Facebook:    Chris Bertish – I'Mpossible
Instagram:  @chrisbertish
Twitter:     @ChrisBertish
LinkdIn:    Chris Bertish
Web:        www.chrisbertish.com
Web:        www.chrisbertishfoundation.org – *a 501(c)(3) registered charity*

Front cover images by Marco Bava and Craig Kolesky
Back cover image by Craig Kolesky
Cover design by JP Redman
Edited by Jacqui L'Ange
Typeset by MR Design
Proofread by Russell Clarke & Robbie Stammers

Printed in the USA
CPSIA information can be obtained
at www.ICGtesting.com
LVHW051103261023
762202LV00005B/137